INGRID NEWKIRK

A BIOGRAPHY OF PETA's FOUNDER

JON HOCHSCHARTNER

Mechanicsburg, PA USA

Published by Sunbury Press, Inc.
Mechanicsburg, Pennsylvania

www.sunburypress.com

For information about special discounts for bulk purchases, please contact Sunbury Press Orders Dept. at (855) 338-8359 or orders@sunburypress.com.

To request one of our authors for speaking engagements or book signings, please contact Sunbury Press Publicity Dept. at publicity@sunburypress.com.

ISBN: 978-1-62006-018-6 (Trade Paperback)

Library of Congress Control Number: 2019931395

FIRST SUNBURY PRESS EDITION: January 2019

Product of the United States of America
0 1 1 2 3 5 8 13 21 34 55

Set in Bookman Old Style
Designed by Crystal Devine
Cover by Terry Kennedy
Edited by Lawrence Knorr

Continue the Enlightenment!

To my daughter Ami, one of my favorite animals.

CONTENTS

1

FLESH OF THE LONG PIGS

Ingrid Newkirk came into the world on June 11, 1949. Born Ingrid Ward, the co-founder of People for the Ethical Treatment of Animals was the only child of Mary Patricia Ward and Noel Oswald Wodehouse Ward. According to Mary's obituary in *The Register-Guard*, Ingrid's mother "lived a hard life as one of the many impoverished children growing up in 1920s London. She served in the British Land Army during WWII, where she met and married her husband."

In a 1990 article, *People* magazine identified Mary as a social worker and Noel as a navigational engineer. They kept a variety of animals, including "dogs, cats, chipmunks, mongooses and exotic birds." The couple moved across the world throughout their daughter's childhood, so it's perhaps unsurprising to read Ingrid say, in a 2009 blog post on PETA's website, that she was conceived in Denmark. According to *Voices from the Underground*, a book by Michael Tobias, Ingrid was born at Kingston upon Thames in England.

Shaan Butters, the author of *That Famous Place*, a history of the town, provided some background about the location. "It was mainly a prosperous place to live with a flourishing local economy and low unemployment," she said in an interview with this writer. "Though perhaps best known as a shopping center, with many jobs in retail, it also continued to have a strong industrial base, grounded in light engineering."

PETA's co-founder spent her early years in this area of Greater London. In a 2017 interview with *The Surrey Comet*, Ingrid struggled to remember her time there. "It's hazy," she said. "I'm 68 and that was 60 years ago. But it's home. If I was a salmon and I spawned, that's where I would go." Ingrid managed to recall some details of her life in Kingston. "I remember always at Christmas we would go to Bentalls [a department store] and ride the train to the North Pole. And we would go to Richmond Park; my father's sister rode a horse there and we would go meet her."

In her book *Making Kind Choices*, Ingrid described some of the gifts her globetrotting father purchased for her. "When I was six, my favorite shoes were a pair of beaded moccasins from an Indian reservation in Canada, which were about five sizes too large for my tiny feet, not that this stopped me from flopping about the house in them, and my favorite doll wore a butterfly-patterned kimono," she wrote. "I would hold her on my lap and read to her about a little boy who ran as fast as he could to escape a tidal wave, a story in the big book my father had brought back from Japan."

The local schools that Ingrid may have attended generally had a good reputation. "In 1951 there were seven local authority primary schools within Kingston Borough, some of them church schools," Butters told this writer, adding there were a few independent preparatory schools as well. "Schools in the period 1949-1956 usually adhered to traditional teaching methods: learning times tables in arithmetic and spellings in English off by heart. There would also usually be a morning assembly containing a short act of Christian worship, where a hymn was sung and prayers said."

PETA's co-founder became deeply bonded with an Irish Red Setter named Shawnie. "He was there when I was born," Ingrid told *Essential Surrey* in a 2015 article. "I was an only child and he was like a brother to me: sometimes we slept together in his wicker basket, and we went in the car together and always got car sick at the same time." Following her father's career, Ingrid moved with her family to New Delhi, India—when she was seven or eight years old, depending on the source.

"We went on the *Cunard Princess* and I thought that Shawnie, who was very old and grey-whiskered, was going to follow," she said in the same *Essential Surrey* piece. "I was told he was going to get his jabs for shipment. I put a ribbon in his hair and we had our pictures taken, but I never saw him again . . . I only found out in adulthood that he had been put down."

The move to India represented quite a change for the young girl, as she related in a 2012 column in *The McCallen Monitor*. "The culture that I was used to was completely different from that of the other children," Ingrid wrote. "So was what I wore, my skin color, my language and much of my behavior. The other children didn't understand when I tried to communicate with them. In one remote village, a boy came up and poked my skin with a stick."

Mary threw herself into charity work, as the future crusader for animals told *Essential Surrey* in 2015. "She was always going to Mother Teresa's orphanage in Old Delhi, where she would make simple cotton toys for the children," Ingrid said, "She also set up a stall at the British embassy, selling handicrafts to benefit the orphanage. She rolled bandages and packed pills for a leper colony and did charity work for unwed mothers because they were ostracized."

Ingrid seems to have accompanied her mother on some of these outings. "There was a big riot when we first arrived and lots of people were killed at a railway station in Calcutta, so children were shipped to the orphanage in Old Delhi," PETA's co-founder said in the *Essential Surrey* interview. "I played with them and my mother and the nuns looked after their wounds."

When she was nine years old, Ingrid witnessed an incident of animal abuse that stayed with her for decades. Susan Reed, the author of the aforementioned *People* magazine article, wrote that Ingrid "looked out the kitchen window of her home and saw an emaciated bullock struggling to pull a heavy cart up the hill. As the animal faltered, its angry owner hit it mercilessly with a long wooden stick. The exhausted bullock stopped in protest. As Ingrid watched in horror, the owner jumped off the cart, lifted the animal's tail and stuck the pole up its rectum, jolting the beast forward." The young girl ran outside and pulled the stick away from the man.

In a 2013 article in *The Times of India*, Ingrid recounted another early exposure in New Delhi to violence against animals. "I remember hearing a group of men laughing in the alley behind my parents' house. They had tied and muzzled a dog to be left for dead in the hot sun solely for their amusement. I went out and rescued the dog but it was too late. It died in our yard."

In September of 1960, Ingrid began classes at Ware Grammar School for Girls, now known as Presdales School, in England. The institutions' records show she previously attended The Convent of Jesus and Mary in New Delhi—according to Fiona Newbold, examinations officer and librarian at Presdales. Ingrid went to Ware

Grammar School for only a few months, until December of 1960, at which point she returned to India.

David Perman, the author of *A New History of Ware*, described the school in an interview with this writer. "It was for day girls only," he said. "Ware Grammar School was a state school. It was run by Hertfordshire County Council, which was quite a progressive educational authority. There was the teaching of religion, but it was taught as a subject. So the school was not affiliated to any church or religious denomination." Students generally knew each other prior to entering Ware Grammar School. "Ingrid would have found herself as a stranger," Perman told this author. "Whether she made friends quickly, we don't know."

Ingrid's pre-activist life is obviously less well documented than her career as a public figure. For instance, in the previously mentioned blog post on PETA's website, she talks about going to school in France and the Orkney Islands. But it's unclear which institutions she's discussing or when exactly she attended them. This writer has heard that, in India, Ingrid went to Presentation Convent in Kodaikanal and Tara Hall in Shimla. But he's been unable to find reliable sourcing to that effect. (Requests to interview Ingrid for this book were unsuccessful.)

What is known is PETA's co-founder had a miserable experience in at least one Catholic boarding institution. "I was the only British girl in this school," Ingrid said in a 2003 profile in *The New Yorker*. "I was hit constantly by nuns, starved by nuns. The whole God thing was shoved right down my throat." In the foreword to PETA's *Vegan College Cookbook*, she recalled being served a meal called pepper water. "I went to school in a totally scary boarding convent run by mean nuns who dressed like Darth Vader and gave us food that was like something from a prison," she wrote. "It's a wonder any of us survived."

In 1967, when Ingrid was approximately 18 years old, she and her family moved to Eglin Air Force Base in the United States, according to the *People* magazine piece. Michael Specter, the author of *The New Yorker* profile, wrote that, while at the Florida military installation, Ingrid's father "helped design bombing systems for airplanes and ships."

In February of that year, presumably shortly after the Wards arrived, *The Fort Walton Beach Playground Daily News* published a photo of Ingrid and her mother attending a meeting of an exotic food group. Apparently involving herself in the local community,

Mary donated to an Easter buffet for servicemen, according to a March article from the same source.

Reed wrote that Ingrid met her husband, race-car driver Steve Newkirk, while in Florida. The co-founder of PETA reminisced to Specter about the first time Steve took her to Watkins Glen International to see a Formula One competition. "I can still remember the smell of the first trip," she said. "At that time, you had to use Castrol motor oil. And the smell of that oil was just divine. They don't use that formula anymore. But I wish they did." Explaining the sport's appeal, an enduring passion for her, Ingrid compared racing to sex. "The first time you hear them rev their engines, my God!" She said. "That noise goes straight up my spine. It's so electrifyingly glorious."

The *People* article suggests Ingrid married Steve in 1968, taking his name. Apparently, children weren't on the agenda, as she was sterilized a few years later, according to Specter. "I am not only uninterested in having children," Ingrid said in *The New Yorker* profile. "I am opposed to having children. Having a purebred human baby is like having a purebred dog; it is nothing but vanity, human vanity." Whether this was the original reasoning behind her decision is unclear.

In 1970, Ingrid and Steve moved to Maryland, where Ingrid began studying to be a stockbroker. But in 1972, when Ingrid was 22 years old, she had a life-changing experience. Her neighbor had abandoned about a dozen cats, who Ingrid brought to the local animal shelter. "When I arrived at the shelter, the woman said, 'Come in the back and we will just put them down there,'" Ingrid recalled to Specter. "I thought, how nice—you will set them up with a place to live. So I waited out front for a while, and then I asked if I could go back and see them, and the woman just looked at me and said, 'What are you talking about? They are all dead.'"

Ingrid was shocked, having been unfamiliar with the shelter worker's euphemism. "I just snapped when I heard those kittens were dead," Ingrid said in *The New Yorker* article. "The woman was so rude. The place was a junk heap in the middle of nowhere. It couldn't have been more horrible. For some reason, and even now I don't know what it was, I decided I needed to do something about it. So I thought, I'm going to work here. I went to see the manager, and he said, 'We have one opening in the kennel.' I asked to have it." The manager assented and the following day Ingrid quit her brokerage job.

While working at the shelter, PETA's co-founder continued to be horrified by the way in which it was run. "I went to the front office all the time, and I would say, 'John is kicking the dogs and putting them into freezers,'" Ingrid told Specter. "Or I would say, 'They are stepping on the animals, crushing them like grapes, and they don't care.' In the end, I would go to work early, before anyone got there, and I would just kill the animals myself. Because I couldn't stand to let them go through that. I must have killed a thousand of them, sometimes dozens every day. Some of those people would take pleasure in making them suffer."

The grim task Ingrid set for herself and the reasons she felt it was necessary took a psychic toll on her. "Driving home every night, I would cry just thinking about it," Ingrid said in *The New Yorker* piece. "And I just felt, to my bones, this cannot be right. I hadn't thought about animal rights in the broader sense. Not then, or even for a while after. But working at that shelter I just said to myself, 'What is wrong with human beings that we can act this way?'"

Ingrid seems not to have lasted long in the job. In April of 1972, *The Washington Post* reported she had been fired after protesting conditions in the facility. "The directors of the county humane society met for five hours Thursday with the two former employees to discuss their charges," LaBarbara Bowman, the article's author, wrote. "The closed-door meeting, attended by 22 members of the board of directors, was marked by yelling and shouting while the board talked with the two women, Ingrid Newkirk, who was fired Wednesday, and Susan Gordon, who resigned last week because she is expecting a baby."

Ingrid and her colleague had already written to a member of the state legislature about animals' treatment in the shelter. Mary Gardner, vice president of the humane society, was quoted in *The Washington Post* piece, saying she visited the shelter often and never witnessed the behavior Ingrid alleged. "County Executive James P. Gleason announced on Wednesday that he was launching an investigation into the care of animals at the shelter," Bowman wrote. "He indicated that some of the problems may have arisen because the County Council had deleted funds from this year's budget that were to be used to build a new expanded shelter."

Ingrid began working on animal-cruelty cases in Montgomery County, as a deputy sheriff, after her stint at the shelter. "By 1976, she had been placed in charge of the animal-disease-control division of the District of Columbia Commission on Public Health," Specter wrote. It was around 1978 that Ingrid became a vegetarian, according to the *People* piece.

"I came across this little pig who had been abandoned on a farm and was in bad shape," Ingrid told *Essential Surrey*. "He was totally dehydrated and I had to hold his head up at the water pump so that he could drink." That evening, she considered defrosting some pork chops for dinner, when the cognitive dissonance became overwhelming. "How could I be appalled at what had been done to this pig I'd just rescued, yet not register how frightening and awful it must have been for the pigs who became my chops?" Ingrid said. "So I stopped eating animals. I would rather just leave them in peace."

Discussing this transformative experience with *The Surrey Comet*, Ingrid took things a step further, relaying one of her father's stories. "My father was in Borneo when I was small, and he used to come back and talk about the cannibals, and they called human flesh the flesh of the long pigs," she said. "In cannibal language, long pig is human." Ingrid's implication seemed to be there was less difference between cannibalism and eating animals than omnivores might like to believe.

Also in 1978, according to the *People* profile, Ingrid became the first female poundmaster of Washington D.C., at which point she stopped the sale of animals to vivisectionists. "Soon after, she became Director of Cruelty Investigations for the Washington Humane Society," Reed wrote, "where she aggressively prosecuted animal abusers." In what comes across as an illuminating commentary on the time, this meant Ingrid sending a man to jail for ten days for burying six puppies alive.

In 1979, Ingrid established new adoption procedures at the pound, according to an article that appeared in *Pacific Stars and Stripes* in February of that year. "We are interviewing prospective owners to let them know that the adoption of a dog is not a frivolous matter," Ingrid was quoted as saying. The stricter process took 2-3 days and included an inspection of the prospective owner's home, and, when applicable, a check with his or her landlord to ensure animals were welcome, *The Washington Post* reported in a March piece.

Ingrid told the newspaper a recent pound survey had found 24 out of 25 placements were being cared for improperly. "We are attempting to find permanent good homes for the dogs we have here so they will never become public nuisances," Ingrid said to *The Washington Post*. Her changes certainly seem admirable. But the layman wonders to what degree, if any, the new rules discouraged potential adopters, leading to an increased percentage of healthy animals put to death in the pound.

2

BIG FRANKS

1980 was a monumental year in Ingrid's life. She and another activist named Alex Pacheco founded PETA and organized the first World Day for Laboratory Animals protest in the U.S., according to a chronology posted on the organization's website. Further, she divorced her husband, Steve, while keeping his name. "Over time, Newkirk's long days—and twenty arrests for civil disobedience—took a toll on her marriage," Reed explained. Specter asserted the two remained friendly.

Also that year, she read *Animal Liberation*, a book by Peter Singer that is often credited with launching the modern animal-rights movement. "Before, I simply thought that people shouldn't cause animals unnecessary pain," Ingrid told Reed. "I had never thought that maybe they don't belong to us, that they have their own place on the planet."

Besides introducing her to the landmark text, Pacheco pushed Ingrid to become vegan, according to *Monkey Business*, Kathy Snow Guillermo's history of PETA's early efforts. (Attempts to interview Kathy for this book were unsuccessful.) Ingrid recalled what motivated her to change, in a 2017 article printed on the website of Holistic Holiday at Sea. "Someone made fun of me for putting milk in my tea and explained that's why we have a veal calf system—to take the milk," she said.

Less consequentially, in terms of influencing the course of her life, Ingrid was consulted by staffers in the Carter administration about what to do with a turkey roosting on the White House grounds. "Since this is Earth Day and she's just another visiting species, I would hope that people would not do infantile and extremist things such as cavalry-type attacks to get her out of the tree," she was quoted as saying in an April article published in *The Yuma Sun.*

In the summer, a British activist named Kim Stallwood visited the United States, where he drove with Ingrid and Pacheco to two national vegetarian conferences. Stallwood was starving, as his flight had been delayed 12 hours. He asked the pair if they had anything to eat. "I hadn't noticed that next to me in the car was a case of Big Franks, which are canned vegan hot dogs," Stallwood wrote in his excellent autobiography, *Growl.* "From somewhere in the front, Ingrid found an opener, opened the can, and held it out the window as she drained the juice." She tossed him back packets of ketchup.

This seemingly-trivial moment made a lasting impression on Stallwood. "Not only did it seem free-spirited and exotic, but I saw two people who'd not only dedicated themselves to animal rights but had a certain tenacity and style," he recalled in the same source. "I'm also fond of this memory as a reminder of how an organization like PETA, which has now grown into a multi-million-dollar concern, was once vernacular and ad-hoc." (Attempts to interview Stallwood for this book were unsuccessful.)

In August, Ingrid told *The Washington Post* that budgetary pressures were leading to an increased number of animals surrendered to the pound. "We're just swamped," she said. "As the economy has gotten worse, more people than ever before are coming in, saying they can't afford to keep their pet. In the last few years, I've seen a notable increase in this. Now it's a matter of course." Later in the piece, Ingrid went so far as to compare the pound to a slaughterhouse.

Later in the year, a pair of Franciscan monastery brothers were initially denied the opportunity to adopt an animal, after pound employees mistakenly believed they wanted a guard dog. Ingrid seemed annoyed by the coverage this garnered. "Why don't you write about our switch to vegetarian dog food—so that no other animals have to die to feed the ones we have here?" Ingrid asked, according to an October article in *The Washington Post.* "We're not saving dogs at the expense of cows and chickens." Ultimately, the brothers could adopt the dog and decided to participate in events marking International Animal Rights Day, Ingrid said.

The Boston Globe printed a story in January of 1981, in which Ingrid announced that—if necessary—the Washington Humane Society would seek an injunction to prevent the government from killing pigeons to reduce excrement. "Rumor had it," she said, "that this was for the inauguration. The [General Services Administration] denies this, but it is suspicious because the last really significant move against the pigeons happened before Richard Nixon's inauguration, so it seemed that it all might be tied into the GSA's preinaugural preparations."

Later that month, Ingrid was one of a large group of people who received Washingtonian of the Year honors, according to a report published in *The Washington Post* at that time. Over ensuing years, she seems to have frequently mentioned this distinction to reporters. One is unsure if Ingrid did this because of genuine pride or a sense of irony—that she, who became something of a scourge of polite society, was once held up as a civic leader.

During a weekend in Mexico around that time, PETA's co-founders began a romantic relationship. "When Pacheco [first] made it clear his feelings for her were growing stronger, Newkirk didn't take it seriously," Kathy Snow Guillermo wrote in *Monkey Business*. "It was during those days lying on the hot sand and swimming along the reef that Newkirk found, to her surprise, that she had fallen in love."

In the summer of 1981, Ingrid and Pacheco decided it would be useful to learn more about the laboratories they were protesting. Pacheco, who was in his third year at George Washington University, started volunteering at the Institute for Behavioral Research, which was experimenting on primates. "I saw filth caked on the wires of the cages, feces piled in the bottom of the cages, urine and rust encrusting every surface," he wrote in the book *In Defense of Animals*, with the help of Anna Francione. "Twelve of the seventeen monkeys had disabled limbs because of surgical interference (deafferentation) when they were juveniles."

Things only seemed worse the closer he looked. "When I came home in the evenings Ingrid and I agonized about the problem and together considered how best to use the information," he wrote in the aforementioned title. "We knew that I must document everything carefully and that months would have to elapse to show the consistent pattern of behavior and neglect that I was witnessing." Eventually, Pacheco turned over all the information he collected to the authorities, which resulted in the first police raid of a research facility in the U.S.

Authorities confiscated the monkeys, which prompted the question of where the animals would stay. "The National Zoo, the facility most capable of assisting, refused to help," Pacheco wrote in the book. "Local animal shelters, although sympathetic, were not equipped. We were finally forced to adopt the basement of a local activist's home." A vivisectionist at IBR quickly filed a motion seeking the monkeys' return, which was granted. But before the laboratory could regain custody, the animals disappeared.

No one seemed to have a significant doubt about who took the monkeys. "Judge Cahoon late Wednesday afternoon ordered the arrest of Ingrid E. Newkirk, Jean V. Goldenberg, and Miss Lanier, all believed to be connected with the Humane Society in the District of Columbia," stated an unsigned, September article in *The Frederick Post*. Alex appeared to play coy in the piece, suggesting the animals were likely "someplace where there's good weather, to the south or west." The next day, a report appeared in the same source saying Ingrid had turned herself in and been released on personal recognizance.

According to Pacheco's account in the book, the primates were returned on the condition they would not be handed over to IBR. A *Washington Post* article published in late September suggests this might have been the case. "The return of the missing monkeys followed days of hushed and intricate negotiations among county police, prosecutors and a representative of the animal rights groups that have been responsible for the animals' care and were believed to be in contact with those who knew the monkeys' most recent whereabouts," Saundra Saperstein reported.

If such an agreement was made, it was quickly broken. The animals were returned to IBR. In an October article in *The Frederick Post*, Ingrid's lawyer, Edward L. Genn, announced his intention to file an appeal. "Genn refused to discuss in detail the grounds for his motions to return the monkeys to the custody of animal interest groups," Ruth Ellis wrote. "But he said one of the prime arguments would be that Judge Cahoon refused to allow testimony from a primate expert regarding the wellbeing of the animals and why they should not be returned to the research laboratory." The appeal was denied, according to an October report in *The Cumberland News*.

A 1982 effort to change the makeup of a local veterinary oversight board divided animal activists. One of the women arrested in connection to the disappearance of the Silver Spring monkeys, as the animals came to be called, opposed replacing two doctors with consumers on the five-member board. Ingrid was in favor of the change. "I think it is vital that there be lay people on the board of any professional organization," Ingrid told *The Washington Post* in August. "The consumer needs to have a say-so because . . . sometimes it is very hard for a professional society to police itself."

Ingrid argued for calm following the discovery of rabid raccoons in the area, pointing out healthy raccoons are often city dwellers. "They live in the drainage system, at construction sites, in Metro (subway) tunnels," she said to United Press International in an October article published in *The Cumberland Sunday Times*. "I don't think there is a square inch of the city where they don't live . . . They are a natural part of District life and (we) ask residents not to panic." The city was testing as many as 14 raccoons a day, Ingrid continued.

Chas Chiodo was a Florida-based animal activist, who—because his wife worked for an airline company—could fly to demonstrations across the country, free of charge. He said he met Ingrid that year, and after only a few trips up, was planning laboratory break-ins with her. "I don't know why she trusted me," he said in an interview with this author. "I guess it was through word of mouth. Plus, I started a group down in Miami. We called it South Florida Animal Rights Activists. I had that going before I met her. So I guess she figured [I was] one of the real ones."

Claims of PETA's involvement in underground actions didn't surprise Peter Singer. "I don't think it would be breaking news," he told this writer. "Let me just say that I have no direct or personal knowledge of that. I know there were such rumors going around. Certainly, it's well known that they received videotapes from people." The philosopher compared PETA's role—in disseminating stolen information—to Wikileaks.

Apparently, PETA's founders broke up that year. "With little time for anything but work, Newkirk's and Pacheco's personal relationship began to suffer," Kathy wrote in *Monkey Business*. "When the man Newkirk had been seeing before she met Pachecho began calling, she was startled to find that she still cared for him, and she began to question the depth of her feelings for Pacheco."

Jealousy played a role too. "Newkirk discovered that Pacheco had been spending time with a young research assistant from another animal protection organization," Kathy wrote in the same source. "The romance in their relationship ended abruptly. After a round of verbal fireworks, Newkirk threw him out of her house."

Despite having thrown him out, Ingrid ultimately remained near Pacheco. "Pacheco moved in with some PETA volunteers who lived nearby, but again, his and Newkirk's animal rights work came first," Kathy wrote in *Monkey Business*. "The two continued to spend so many hours together that before long Pacheco moved back in—this time as a housemate."

In 1983, economic forces were still resulting in large numbers of animals surrendered to the shelter. A disproportionate number of those surrendered belonged to the elderly. "Old people," Ingrid told *The Washington Post* in February, "have old pets, and there's absolutely no hope for adoption." The shelter wouldn't offer false hope to those surrendering animals. According to the unsigned article, "the shelter now invites elderly people bringing in pets to walk into a back room and be with their pets as the animals are killed."

The New York Times reported in May about a protest against the Fur Expo, which was held at the New York Statler Hotel. While 50 activists protested outside, Ingrid and Chas snuck into the event. Reporters Laurie Johnston and Susan Hellen Anderson wrote the pair of agitators "took over the microphone—after the Fur Expo fashion show and before the banquet—and made a statement. In the ruckus that followed, the police arrived from the Midtown South Precinct station."

The same *New York Times* piece said Ingrid and Chas, representing PETA, swore out complaints of harassment after the incident. "Mr. Chiodo said he had been punched above the eye by a civilian, according to Police Officer John Clifford," Johnston and Anderson wrote. "Miss Newkirk said that her arm had been pinned behind her back." Still, Ingrid seemed to be in good spirits. "The police were a delight and most of the security people were fine and professional," she told the reporters.

In August, *The New York Times* covered the third annual Action for Life conference—an animal-rights gathering, organized at Montclair State University by activist Alex Hershaft. Even by this early date, Ingrid seems to have established quite a reputation within the movement. "Newkirk, director of People for the Ethical Treatment of Animals, was treated like a heroine at the conference," reporter Philip Shenon wrote. "People wanted to shake her hand. They applauded wildly when she spoke."

Later in August, Ingrid was among approximately 300 animal activists who protested the American Psychological Association's convention, at which the chief vivisector in the Silver Spring monkey case had a speaking role. *The Los Angeles Times* covered the event. "The first time you know if something is safe is when it is tested on humans," Ingrid told reporter Peter M. Warren. "Thalidomide (a tranquilizer that caused deformities in the unborn in the 1950s and 1960s) was successfully tested on hundreds of animals from sea urchins to the great ape, yet its potential for birth defects went undetected."

That year, PETA helped shut down a Department of Defense wound lab, according to a post on the group's website about military exploitation of animals. "After PETA exposed and protested the Army's plan to purchase dozens of dogs from animal shelters and shoot them on a firing range in Maryland, the military halted the program and permanently banned the use of dogs, cats, and primates in wound treatment experiments and training," the unsigned piece asserted. An October article in *The Washington Post* described a PETA protest against the program.

Also in October, Ingrid inserted herself into a racial controversy. After Howard Cosell called Alvin Garrett, a black player on the Washington Redskins, 'that little monkey,' Mayor Marion Barry wrote an outraged telegram to the broadcaster. "The Mayor may have a chip on his shoulder," Ingrid was quoted as saying in a piece by Les Kinsolving, published by *The Carrizozo Lincoln County News*. "The monkey is a very clean, intelligent, highly social and sensitive animal that protects his family and doesn't engage in war." Speaking for PETA, Ingrid said the organization didn't regard Cosell's word choice as an insult to Garrett. "The Mayor's statement is unfortunate," she continued. "We are just one animal species."

In November, Ingrid was the subject of a long profile in *The Washington Post*. She had resigned her position as head of the district's animal disease control division the month before. "Newkirk says her decision to leave the District government had nothing to

do with the fact that she championed animal rights while super-
vising the death-by-injection of tens of thousands of animals at
the D.C. Animal Shelter," reporter Chip Brown wrote, suggesting
Ingrid's views—on what is euphemistically described as euthanasia—have garnered criticism since the beginning of her career. "She
says she believed she had 'made all the changes I could at the shelter' and the time had come to spend 'every free moment' working
for animal rights as the director of People for the Ethical Treatment
of Animals."

Brown provided an interesting glimpse into PETA headquarters at the time. "PETA's offices in a ground-floor apartment in
Takoma Park, D.C. also serve as a home for Newkirk, founder Alex
Pachecho . . . a half-deaf watchdog named Bea and two cats who
nap on computers bought with a grant from a Hindu-oriented foundation," he wrote. "One wall poster reproduces the ravaged face of
an orangutan who has been exposed to dioxin. The bookshelves sag
with animal rights tracts and vegetarian cookbooks. The kitchen
refrigerator contains the fixings for meat-free lunches, and there
are plenty of plastic shoe catalogs to thumb through."

While speaking with Brown, Ingrid made a comment that would
be quoted for decades in attempts to discredit her. "Six million
people died in concentration camps, but 6 billion broiler chickens
will die this year in slaughterhouses," she said. "It's very bad to be
afraid of that comparison." Ingrid continued, aware of the reaction
her words could provoke, and unconcerned by it. "Many of the furriers come unglued when we use the word Auschwitz," she said.
"What we're saying is that slaughterhouses are Auschwitzes for
animals. Fur farms are Buchenwalds for animals. Remember that
situation and be upset that 6 billion individuals are going through
those things today, only it's called fried chicken. It was wrong then,
and it's still wrong."

The Washington Post profile had a significant impact on Karen
Davis, the future founder of United Poultry Concerns. "I saved the
article," she told this writer. "I still have it." Karen was deeply impressed by Ingrid's portrayal. "I was so drawn to her arguments
[and] the things she was doing for animals," she said. "It was the
eloquence of her speech. It was her total confidence in her enterprise." Karen believed reading the piece was one of the first times
she was exposed to an animal-rights perspective. "In the United
States, there were only the old, dinosaur organizations," Karen said,
referring to groups like the American Society for the Prevention of

Cruelty to Animals. "They weren't doing anything at all for farmed animals, for example, except eating them."

Eventually, Karen started volunteering at the PETA office. "Ingrid was busy," Karen told this writer. "She was on a mission. She valued us being there. She was looking for good volunteers. She was friendly, but she had a reserve about her too." Sometime in the next few years, Ingrid turned down Karen's request to work professionally for PETA. "She thought I would do better to work on my own," Karen said, "which I took—and still take—to mean her saying that she saw in me something that would most likely not be compliant."

Ingrid strove to project a professional appearance when PETA engaged in picketing. "Probably some people were smoking marijuana," Karen told this writer. "They were dressing maybe too casually. Ingrid didn't like that. She said, when we're out there, we must look good; we must present ourselves well, and we can't be out there doing anything but [focusing] on why we're there. Of course, she's right about that." This caused some resentment. "It does happen, where a volunteer has this attitude—hey, I'm doing you a favor, so don't tell me what to do," Karen said. "I think there was some of that."

In December of 1983, Ingrid served as a spokesperson for the Animal Liberation Front, an underground group dedicated to freeing non-humans and inflicting financial damage on those who exploited them. "The Animal Liberation Front has conducted three Christmas raids—one in California, one in Florida, and one in Maryland," she announced in an Associated Press article published in the *Alamogordo Daily News*. "The ALF wants an end to the suffering of billions of animals in institutions across the country . . . They want to bring the Christmas spirit to animals."

Ingrid insisted she had no inside knowledge of the action, according to a December piece in *The Los Angeles Times*. "Newkirk said she does not know who stole the [laboratory] dogs or how the theft was accomplished," reporter Eric Malnic wrote. "She said that, as in the past, she simply received a call from someone named Jean in the Los Angeles area who reported the thefts and the vandalism."

3

THE ANIMAL
EUTHANASIA FRONT

On a snowy day in January of 1984, PETA members protested in front of a Washington hotel, according to a short piece in *The New York Times*. "Ingrid Newkirk, a spokesman for the group, said the vigil was held in response to the state visit of Prime Minister Zhao Ziyang of China and a recent campaign in Peking in which stray running dogs of Chinese communism were clubbed to death or drowned," writers William E. Farrell and Warren Weaver Jr. stated.

Later in January, PETA accused Texas ranchers of allowing 100 horses to starve to death and falsely claiming cold weather wrecked their pasturage. "This about the freeze is a great big coverup on their part," Ingrid was quoted as saying in a UPI report published in *The Escanaba Daily Press*. "These horses are inconsequential to people who are trying to make a quick buck."

She continued, in the UPI piece, arguing some of the animals—who were supposed to be fattened for slaughter—died quite some time before the cold weather struck. According to the organizational chronology posted on PETA's website, the group shut down a Texas slaughterhouse operation in 1984 that starved its horses. This appears to be the case to which the post is referring.

Ingrid appeared in a June article in *The New York Times*, which attempted to trace the origins of the animal movement and give a sense of its scope. She said those involved in the cause had undergone a significant philosophical change since the mid-1970s. "It's not just 'don't beat dogs' anymore," Ingrid told reporter William Robbins. "For the first time in the United States, people are realizing that animals are creatures, too, and they have rights." She added that PETA, having launched four years prior with a mere 18 members, now had over 23,000 supporters.

Around that time, Chas started working for PETA professionally. "I told them I was willing to pack up, come up there, and work for them," he said in an interview with this writer. "They paid me minimum wage for 40 hours—whatever that was back then. I worked 60-80 hours, but I got paid for the 40 hours. That was okay. I was doing animal-rights work." Chas already knew he didn't like Ingrid. "You wanted to work with her because she was getting stuff done," he recalled, "even though she was not very good to the people who were helping her."

As an example of this, Chas described the unexpected firing of a PETA employee. "I'm thinking about this one woman," he told this author. "[She] sold all of her stuff or packed up and moved to Washington to work for PETA. She lasted a month. Without any feelings at all, Ingrid just fired her." He said this wasn't uncommon during his tenure with the organization. "It was like a swinging door there, sometimes," he said. "There were so many people being hired. Then, suddenly—two weeks, or a month, two months later—they're gone."

Lorri Houston, who would go on to become a co-founder of Farm Sanctuary, argued Ingrid's reputation for toughness wasn't fair. "Would we be saying that if she was a guy?" Lorri asked this writer. "Would we even have that discussion? I don't think so." The Farm Sanctuary co-founder mentioned Richard Morgan, who started Mobilization for Animals, had a hardball approach as well. "You never heard that about him or some of the other folks," Lorri said. "You just wouldn't hear that about guys."

In September, *The Brownsville Herald* published a dispatch from Knight Ridder Newspapers explaining how PETA planned to screen vivisection footage for lawmakers, as part of a congressional hearing on animal research. However, the screening was canceled when legislators discovered the footage had been stolen during an ALF raid. "If the only way to make illegal acts public is to do it in an illegal way, then that's a commendable service," Ingrid told reporter Angelia Herrin. "It's not like anyone has been hurt who didn't deserve it."

In November, *The Globe and Mail* ran a story in which Ingrid disputed a claim that British scientists were moving to the United States to escape regulation. "In the United States, the researchers are paid more," PETA's co-founder explained to journalist Lynne Thomas. "Besides, Britain's scientific reputation hasn't suffered in terms of Nobel Prize triumphs. It is bettered only by that of the United States, where sheer numbers of researchers working more than account for the gain."

That month, a Gibson Island deer hunt was postponed, after PETA threatened to file a court injunction to stop it. In an Associated Press piece, published by *The Annapolis Capital*, Ingrid insisted there were alternatives to the hunt, which was intended to solve an alleged problem of deer overpopulation. Leaders of the private island should "sit down with a wildlife biologist with a humane orientation and try to establish the extent of the overpopulation, and why there is increased interaction between the deer and the residents," Ingrid was quoted as saying in the unsigned article.

In the same source, Ingrid stated PETA was willing to disrupt any organized hunt, though the group hoped it didn't come to that. "If the Gibson Island residents can put out a little money to deter the deer—and they obviously can if they can afford to live there—then there will be no need to kill any of the animals," she said, adding natural barriers could separate animal habitats from human residences, or the deer could be taken to a refuge.

Later in November, the hunt went forward and PETA members protested outside the community's gate. "Newkirk said the Gibson Island Corp. had violated an agreement with PETA and the state Department of Natural Resources to find more humane ways to thin the herd," Johanne Brown wrote in *The Annapolis Capital* at the time. "The DNR has already said PETA's alternatives for thinning the herd would be ineffective and costly." According to a December article in *The Washington Post*, ten deer were killed.

Following an ALF raid in December, which freed approximately 100 animals from City of Hope National Medical Center, Ingrid held a press conference on behalf of the clandestine group, according to a UPI report published in *The Fort Madison Daily Democrat* that month. "Animals are routinely found dead in their fecal matter after being left unattended overnight or over the weekend, and bleed to death alone in their cages," she alleged in the piece, speaking of laboratory conditions.

An Associated Press article, published by *The Nashua Telegraph* in December, indicates Ingrid crashed a news conference held by City of Hope, causing the event to devolve into a shouting match. Ten rabbits—believed to have been among those rescued —ended up being seized by police, after a suspected member of the ALF was arrested, a December piece in *The Los Angeles Times* stated. Still, according to the chronology on PETA's website, the government suspended more than $1 million in federal funding to the laboratory due to its treatment of animals.

In 1985, Ingrid ran into Neal Barnard, who had recently created the Physicians Committee for Responsible Medicine. "While driving down the congested Wisconsin Avenue in Bethesda, Md., Barnard saw a few demonstrators waving anti-fur posters in front of a department store," Kathy wrote in *Monkey Business*. "How pitiful, he thought. How could so few activists hope to influence anybody? He swerved his car into an open space; at least he could lend a hand. This was how, quite unexpectedly, Barnard met PETA's national director, Ingrid Newkirk." Speaking with this writer, Chas recalled the pair beginning a romantic relationship around that time.

In April, an unsigned article appeared in *The Tyrone Daily Herald*, which allowed Ingrid to promote an upcoming rally against vivisection. "We are going to bring it home to the University of Pennsylvania," she said, referencing experiments on primates that took place at the school. "The animals are not anesthetized and they treat the animals with enormous disrespect." Ingrid added videotapes of the experiments in question, performed by the Head Injury Clinical Research Center, would be available at the rally.

These tapes had been taken in an earlier ALF raid of the University of Pennsylvania medical school. "Copies of the tapes were turned over to the U.S. Agriculture Department last week and it pledged to conduct a fair investigation into the experiments at the university, [Ingrid] said," according to *The Tyrone Daily Herald* piece. "The tapes have also been the center of an investigation by the Philadelphia district attorney's office to learn how PETA obtained the tapes."

In July, *The Philadelphia Daily News* ran a story about PETA occupations of NIH offices, which was called off after the

Health and Human Services secretary suspended funding to the University of Pennsylvania's Head Injury Clinical Research Center. "[Approximately 70 activists] had taken over the offices of two undersecretaries Monday while supporters camped outside, holding up banners and showing excerpts of the videotapes taken during the raid at the Penn lab," reporters Ann W. O'Neill and Kitty Caparella wrote. "Last night, group members—rested and showered after their four-day protest—celebrated at a vegetarian dinner party in Silver Spring, Md."

In the same *Philadelphia Daily News* story, Ingrid defended the ALF's theft of tapes from the University of Pennsylvania. "I wish there had been another way to do it without necessitating a break-in," she said, before arguing the ends justified the means. "In this case, those baboons think so and I think so and every taxpayer and every human being with a grain of compassion should think so."

In October, *The Syracuse Post Standard* covered a lecture Ingrid gave at Cornell University about animal experimentation. "We have no right to kill an animal or cause them pain to ensure our survival," Ingrid said. "When people argue that there is a benefit in the use of animals, we challenge the very premise of that statement . . . To say that something is beneficial does not justify exploitation." Reporter Brian G. Bourke wrote Ingrid predicted the end of animal agriculture within 40 years, which drew laughter from the crowd.

While protesting a Woodward & Lothrop fur sale at the Mayflower Hotel, Ingrid was one of 15 people arrested and charged with disorderly conduct, according to a December article in *The Washington Post*. "There is a Christmas sale inside which we think is totally inappropriate," she was quoted as saying by Eugene L. Meyer. "At this time of year, people are supposed to show compassion."

In his book *Eco-terrorism*, Don Liddick asserted PETA donated $60,000 to the legal defense of ALF activist Roger Troen in 1986, who was arrested in connection with a raid on the University of Oregon. Ingrid wrote in her text *Free the Animals* that PETA hired attorney Steven Houze to represent Troen. Ultimately, the defendant was convicted of burglary, theft, and conspiracy, according to Dean Kuiper's book *Operation Bite Back*.

According to Josh Harper—the animal-rights campaigner who would go on to archive the movement's history at the Talon

Conspiracy website —Roger gave information to authorities which resulted in several activists being arrested. "Ingrid continued to support him over the years, to defend him, to make claims that those [Freedom of Information Act] documents were fake and some attempt at counterintelligence by the FBI," Josh told this author. "But I find that doubtful."

Beginning around the time of PETA's contribution to Roger's legal defense, the relationship between Ingrid's organization and a newer generation of ALF activists was becoming strained. "I don't think that it's much of a secret that PETA was helping to re-home animals," Josh said in an interview with this writer, referring to nonhumans illegally rescued from laboratories. "They had been entrusted to do that by people who believed that those animals were going to go on to live good lives—inside of homes. My understanding from speaking to a lot of these activists is that's not what occurred." Instead, the nonhumans were put to death.

As this became known among underground circles, a disparaging nickname for Ingrid's organization was born. "A lot of the more youthful Animal Liberation Front activists at the time started referring to PETA, and ALF activists that were working on some level with PETA, as the Animal Euthanasia Front," Josh told this author, adding some members of the newer generation resented PETA's co-founder acting as the ALF's spokesperson. "There was definitely an internal split where a lot of people did not want Ingrid to be involved anymore."

Kim Bartlett, a movement journalist, believed Ingrid visited her in Texas in the early part of 1986. "I arranged some speaking opportunities, one or more interviews on local television, [and] some radio spots," Bartlett told this writer. "I didn't feel that it was hard to get close to her. From my point of view, we had sort of an instant bond." This connection seems to have been based on their shared commitment to the nonhuman cause. "We both talked about how we'd really like to just go live at the beach and enjoy life," Bartlett recalled. "And yet, we couldn't enjoy life because of how animals were suffering. It tore at us. It tore at our souls. We both had a catalyzing event or series of events, and we couldn't look back."

According to a Knight Ridder piece, printed in April by *The Colorado Springs Gazette-Telegraph*, police confiscated a cow from Hershaft, which he intended to use as a prop for a demonstration. Farm

Animal Rights Movement had apparently transported the nonhuman in a closed truck in 80-degree heat. "I called Ingrid and she gave me the scolding of my life," Hershaft told this writer, noting she accused him of betraying the cause. "I felt pretty horrible back then. I knew what it felt like to be hounded out of the movement." However, Roger Galvin, a PETA attorney, offered some words of comfort.

Speaking with this writer, Hershaft, Chas, and *Animal Factories* coauthor Jim Mason said they heard Ingrid dated the lawyer at one point. Karen Davis recalled hearing this too, though she had trouble imagining it. "Roger is a very stolid kind of guy," Karen told this writer. "He was a great guy. But he was not somebody you would picture in a romantic situation. I can't picture him and Ingrid together, but I know that in our movement—like amongst people everywhere and all kinds of organizations—people have affairs with all kinds of other people, who are at that moment in the same enterprise."

In May, *The Washington Post* published a piece by Ingrid, in which she called on the National Institutes of Health to release the Silver Spring monkeys, apparently to Primarily Primates sanctuary in Texas. "The issue, in this case, is not one of monkeys versus man or one of eliminating the use of all animals in research," Ingrid wrote. "Those red herrings are intended merely to deflect attention from the issue at hand." This, she continued, was the NIH wasting taxpayer money, disrespecting activists who exposed the monkey's abuse, and leaving the animals in isolation for no reason.

A vivisector expressed concern about his work drawing the attention of the ALF, in a June profile in *The Washington Post*. Ingrid, who said she spoke on behalf of the underground group, offered no reassurance. "He should be worried," Ingrid told reporter Phil McCombs. "No one knows what they [the Front] are going to do. We learn after the fact. But they rescue lots of animals, who thank them very much."

That summer, Bartlett started working for PETA professionally. "The idea was that I was coming to Washington for a few months, and then I was going to open up the California office," the movement journalist recalled to this writer. "That was to be my role. But I didn't last at PETA more than about six weeks." The job was not what she imagined. "I wanted Ingrid to look at what I'd done," Bartlett recalled. "I got her at a bad moment and she just sort of unloaded on me."

This occurred in front of Bartlett's coworkers. "I felt utterly humiliated and very angry," the movement journalist said in an interview with this writer. "She's smart enough to figure out everybody's weak spots." Bartlett promptly quit PETA and accepted an offer to serve as editor of *The Animals' Agenda*. "I had what I learned to call the Ingrid Experience, which was Ingrid losing her temper," the movement journalist said. "She could be a little bit vicious."

Looking back, Bartlett was more sympathetic to Ingrid. "I think a lot of it had to do with stress and the difficulties of trying to start an organization," the movement journalist said. "She did everything. She was the brains behind it—and yet she ended up being the person who had to take out the trash and clean it up on the weekends." Ingrid and Pacheco were living in their offices at the time. "It was all-consuming," Bartlett said. "Alex was sort of a laid-back person. He didn't absorb the stress as Ingrid did."

In August, Ingrid seems to have been part of a group of protesters who were arrested after staging a sit-in outside the Department of Health and Human Services, a UPI report published in *The Defiance Crescent News* said. The activists demanded an audience with the HHS secretary as part of an effort to release the Silver Spring monkeys. "We want the public to know that the National Institutes of Health sees animals as disposable garbage," Ingrid was quoted as saying in the unsigned piece. The protestors had held a vigil outside NIH for the previous 100 days.

Later that month, *The New York Times* ran a piece on the ideological division within the animal-protection movement, following conflict at The Humane Society of the United States (HSUS) about whether to regulate or abolish vivisection. Ingrid argued groups like her own inspired such debates in traditionally-conservative organizations. "The new blood doesn't think that the old blood knows what it's doing," she said. "And very often the old blood has forgotten what the purpose of the organization is all about."

Chas was among a group of workers who decided to leave PETA that summer. In an interview with this writer, he said Ingrid tried to convince him to stay, but he told her he could no longer tolerate how she treated people. "Then she said, Chas, do you know what the problem with you is?" The activist from Florida recalled. "[Ingrid said], Chas, you have too many friends; I don't want any friends; I don't need any friends, and I don't have any close friends."

A significant number of people left with Chas. "It was like a mutiny," he told this author. "There were about 10-12 of us who all quit." The group went to the next meeting of PETA volunteers to explain why they were leaving. "A couple of days earlier, we were heroes to them," Chas said. "Then they were hissing and booing us at the meeting because we were coming down on Ingrid and Alex. The volunteers were still looking at them like they were gods."

A U.S. appeals court refused to release the Silver Spring monkeys, saying PETA had no standing to sue, according to a UPI article that appeared in *The Independence Examiner* in September. "We are convinced we are right," Ingrid said, promising to appeal the decision to the U.S. Supreme Court if need be. "If we can just break a little new ground and get beyond the conservative viewpoint on this issue then I'm sure the rights of animals are going to be recognized."

In October, *The Wall Street Journal* ran a piece in which Ingrid responded to a fur-industry advertisement campaign, featuring the slogans 'Fur is for Life' and 'An Industry in Harmony with Nature.' "If one wishes to think of 'harmony with nature' as being bludgeoned and slaughtered, then I guess they're right," she told reporter Jolie Solomon. "But fur is death, no matter how you cloak it."

As director of PETA and a spokesperson for the ALF, sometimes it was unclear for which group Ingrid was speaking. That was the case, for instance, in a Knight Ridder News Service piece published in December in *The Madison Wisconsin State Journal*. "We show no deference to property in our efforts to protect animals," Ingrid told reporter Michael Zielenziger, whose article highlighted tactical disagreements between environmental groups like Greenpeace and the Sea Shepherd Conservation Society. At a glance, the divide between PETA and the ALF seemed less stark.

Following the liberation of four chimpanzees from a SEMA laboratory by an underground organization, Ingrid argued NIH deserved blame for the researcher's abuse of animals, according to a December report in *The Frederick News-Post*. "NIH has got to take some responsibility and decide why they are allowing these animals to die from things like having their foot caught in cages and starving," she told reporter Sonia Boin, adding AIDS research SEMA conducted was both cruel and ineffective. The chronology on PETA's website indicated the organization's campaigning got the laboratory to stop using isolation chambers.

Later in December, *The Washington Post* ran a largely-sympathetic profile of a furrier who had recently opened a store in the area. Ingrid was quoted in the piece, slamming the merchant. "The way he glamorizes what is a barbaric industry which causes enormous cruelty to animals is very offensive," she said to journalist Stephanie Mansfield. "I think he's chosen the wrong town to come to. People in Washington are more attuned to the growing awareness of animal rights."

Ingrid planned to spend Christmas at the zoo, according to a brief article in *The New York Times* that was published the day of the celebration. "Today, when most Americans are probably preparing for a Christmas meal of turkey or perhaps a roast goose, a group of vegetarians will be singing Christmas carols and making gifts of exotic fruits and nuts to the primates in the National Zoo," Irvin Molotsky and Robin Toner wrote. The facility, traditionally closed during the holiday, cooperated in the endeavor. "We give them a little bit of family on Christmas," Ingrid told the reporters. "We're primates, too."

4

COOL, SHREWD SAVVY

In January of 1987, *The Wall Street Journal* printed a letter from Ingrid, in which she countered the notion that anti-vivisectionist groups, like PETA, were akin to Luddites. "Our membership includes physicians, scientists and health-care professionals who are concerned that good science is often crushed by grant seekers with little talent and fewer scruples," she wrote. "PETA vigorously promotes the use of non-animal methodologies that represent the leading edge of science, from the cloning of human skin cells for toxicology and burns research to the most sophisticated computer models of living systems."

In February, Stallwood left the British Union for the Abolition of Vivisection to serve as PETA's executive director. He seems to have played a large role in professionalizing the American group. "I made sure that not only was the organization's management restructured, but that there were written monthly reports, planning meetings each week, and biannual retreats," Stallwood wrote in his autobiography. "I supervised the complete reorganization of the finances, including the creation of a new, computerized accounting system, financial reports, and twenty departmental budgets."

Jim Mason didn't seem to think it was a coincidence that two British activists—Ingrid and Stallwood —were leading PETA. "It always seemed a little weird," he told this author. "But everyone in our movement knows that the English are quite a bit ahead of us on the animal issue. The first SPCA was in England, decades before the United States. The English culture gave birth to the ALF and the hunt saboteurs. The English have always been much more radical and much more active across the board." Jim also suggested British media might have influenced PETA's attention-seeking tactics. "England is home of the scandalous tabloid bullshit," he said. "So Ingrid and Kim knew how to work that."

Bartlett recalled speaking with Ingrid around that time, to clear the air between them. "Cleveland Amory, the founder of the Fund for Animals and a well-known writer, had invited me and Doug Moss, who was the publisher of *The Animals' Agenda*, to come to a meeting in his office in New York City," she told this author, noting Ingrid and Stallwood were there. "*The Animals' Agenda* was the publication of record for the animal-rights movement. It was very important. Of course, PETA was the prominent organization." For this reason, Cleveland believed Bartlett and Ingrid needed to re-solve their differences.

While nothing inflammatory was said, Bartlett described the conversation as somewhat tense. Besides their personal conflict, she and Ingrid had substantive disagreements on strategy. "At *Animals' Agenda*, we were very devoted to this philosophy of print-ing all the news and all the criticism," Bartlett told this writer. "We felt that was essential to the growth of the movement and to the integrity of the movement. So we weren't going to back down if we had a problem with how PETA was doing something." The meeting offered no real resolution.

In April of 1987, Ingrid was quoted in an *Orlando Sentinel* story, arguing inadequate federal laboratory inspections justified ALF raids. "The ALF has turned out to be the only trustworthy inspector of labs in the U.S.," she told reporter Lisanne Renner. "Not one of the closed facilities that the ALF raided would be closed today if it wasn't for the ALF."

In May, *The Globe and Mail* began a series on the animal movement, in which Ingrid spoke eloquently about humans' often contradic-tory view of animals. "We have ethical epilepsy when it comes to our attitude about animals," she said. "The two parts of our brain aren't linked together. We love them, we put them on our nursery walls, we make stuffed toys, we teach our children to be kind . . . and then there's this terrible other world—of experimentation and slaugh-ter—that goes on behind closed doors." Surprisingly, the second article in the series claimed Ingrid supported subsistence hunting.

That same month, *The Nashua Telegraph* published a Scripps Howard News Service piece, in which Ingrid appeared to condone an arson attack on a California laboratory. "I'd rather it had happened in a different way," she said. "But I'm glad that lab isn't going to be there. It would have been used to torture non-human primates." Ingrid continued, arguing such attacks were inevitable. "If this one wasn't done by the Animal Liberation Front, they'll do something like it sooner or later as their frustration wells up and flows over," she said. "As long as labs are closed fortresses, those kinds of actions will be necessary."

When researchers tasked with monitoring the Silver Spring monkeys recommended eight of the animals be put to death, claiming it was the compassionate thing to do, Ingrid opposed the suggestion. This was somewhat surprising, given her demonstrated willingness to do the same to healthy cats and dogs. "We want people who care about them taking care of them for the rest of their lives—they've been through hell and back," Ingrid said in an article that ran in *The New York Times* later that month. She added activists had been prevented from seeing the monkeys. "They have not been able to touch human beings," Ingrid stated. "We used to be able to visit, take fruit, at least groom them. Now they just sit in metal boxes."

After a legislator convinced the San Diego Zoo to take in some of the Silver Spring monkeys, Ingrid worried the government would kill the remaining animals. "Newkirk is afraid that NIH will use the separation of the monkeys as an excuse to put the nine left behind to death, and rid itself of a lingering, embarrassing problem," Robin Goldstein wrote in a June piece in *The Orange County Register*. "People for the Ethical Treatment of Animals has agreed to pay all the costs to send the monkeys to Primarily Primates, but has been rebuffed by the government, according to Newkirk."

An Associated Press report—published by *The Cumberland News* in August—said PETA was behind a raid on a Maryland laboratory that rescued many animals. Whether or not PETA members were involved in the effort, reporter Lisa M. Hamm seems to have misunderstood Ingrid's nominal relationship to underground groups like the Animal Liberation Front. "People for the Ethical Treatment of Animals, an animal rights group, on Monday claimed responsibility for the break-in," Hamm wrote. Such confusion seemed bound to happen, given the tightrope Ingrid was walking.

Carol Helstosky, who was hired by PETA at the end of the summer, said Ingrid required all her employees to complete a ride-along with an animal-control officer. "It was really important for her for us to understand how animals could be so throwaway," Helstosky told this writer. "I gained a kind of respect—maybe a grudging respect, I'm not really sure—for the people who had to mop this up."

Around that time, some of the staff feared the organization's relationship with the ALF had resulted in government surveillance. "There were always rumors about maybe someone who worked at PETA was an undercover FBI agent," Helstosky said in an interview with this writer. "I don't recall anyone being fired abruptly because of that suspicion. But I do remember people talking about that." For her part, Helstosky believed authorities had more important things to do. "I wasn't really clear that the FBI was taking it that seriously," she said. "Maybe that was naïve of me. I'm not sure."

According to an Associated Press report, published in October by *The New Bern Sun-Journal*, Ingrid cheered a decision by East Carolina University to place a one-year moratorium on the use of dogs in basic-sciences courses. "ECU officials have a chance in the 12 months to really prove that they are a progressive school and that they are interested in the humane treatment of their students and the animals," she said. The decision seems to have been made because of activist pressure. "ECU's action came a little more than a month after PETA representatives charged at a news conference in Washington D.C. that a videotape of a dog undergoing surgery in an ECU laboratory showed that the animal had not been properly anesthetized," the unsigned report stated.

That year, PETA took over the New England Anti-Vivisection Society, according to professor Harold D. Guither. "Alex Pacheco and Ingrid Newkirk, codirectors of PETA, joined the board," he wrote in his book *Animal Rights*, adding the founder of Fund for Animals became NEAVS' president. "Other board members included Dr. Neal Barnard of the Physicians Committee for Responsible Medicine and Theo Capaldo, a member of the NEAVS-funded Psychologists for the Ethical Treatment of Animals. Funds were liberally dispersed to groups and projects aligned with PETA and Fund for Animals."

In an interview with this writer, Jim Mason argued PETA's takeover of NEAVS was necessary. "We were coming into activism when we realized that all the old groups—the established groups—were asleep at the wheel," he said, speaking in generational terms. "They weren't doing anything except keeping their friends and family on

the payroll. And that was especially true of all the AV societies."
Bartlett agreed, describing NEAVS as ineffective prior to the takeover. "Some funds had been misused," the movement journalist
recalled. "It was an organization that had a lot of money."

Perhaps it was around this time that Ingrid invited Peter Singer
to address her staff. "PETA was taking over another animal organization, which caused some concern in the animal movement," the
philosopher told this writer, adding he mentioned the issue when
speaking to Ingrid's employees. "I think that she was a little disappointed that I had addressed that question. She thought it wasn't
perhaps the best thing I could have done on the occasion—that it
might have unsettled PETA staff or something of that sort. She had
hoped I would be more inspirational to them."

Jim suspected Ingrid had set up PETA's board, which was com-
prised of a small group of loyalists, so her organization couldn't be
taken over. "It wasn't like she had any kind of quasi-democratic
structure to the leadership," he told this writer. "Some of the new-
comers get ambitious. They think the old fart that started the group
needs to be retired. I think Ingrid saw a few of these situations and
tried to arrange things so that it couldn't happen." Jim seemed
impressed by this. "It's just a measure of Ingrid's savvy—her really
cool, shrewd savvy—that she would know how to exploit the vulnerabilities of another group," he said, "and at the same time make her
own group not have those vulnerabilities."

Speaking with this author, Jon Bockman, executive director of
Animal Charity Evaluators, expressed serious reservations about
groups with small, subservient boards. "That's a real disservice to
the organization," he said. "You're not getting that earnest, honest,
sincere feedback. You're not getting that group of advisors to tell
you that this is a bad idea . . . It's just an echo chamber, reinforcing
whatever ideas the executive director has."

In November of 1987, *The Los Angeles Times* published a piece
about the Silver Spring monkeys, in which Ingrid reflected on the
legacy and impact of their saga. "The case frightened people in the
experimentation community," she told reporter Janny Scott. "It's a
symbol to them of impending change and perhaps the end of a century of absolutely unfettered animal use." Ingrid continued, arguing
the affair helped launch the U.S. animal rights movement. "Before
that, there had been very, very small groups, mostly individuals

who didn't know where other people who shared their convictions were," she said. "There was no movement as such."

In an email interview with this author, Merritt Clifton, a movement journalist, argued Ingrid's handling of the Silver Spring monkey case demonstrated her promotional ingenuity. "Similar cases involving Trans-Species Unlimited and Mobilization for Animals (the Pennsylvania head injury clinic) and Last Chance for Animals (an undercover exposé of the facility that became notorious later for the Baby Fae heart transplant case) involved most of the same elements and occurred within the same time frame, but did not kindle publicity to anywhere near the same extent, and did not result in the same sort of rapid organizational growth," he wrote. "To me, this illustrates a combination of luck and Newkirk's superior ability to capitalize on luck with successful fundraising and media campaigns."

In 1988, Ingrid was frustrated after visiting a Department of Agriculture research lab, according to an Associated Press article published by *The Sedalia Democrat* that February. "Our tour was not an honest tour, and we were not able to get answers to very simple questions," she told reporter Don Kendall. "We were told (before the visit) that we could see the areas that we would want to see. It was disappointing, to say the least." A spokesperson for the laboratory was quoted in the piece, claiming Ingrid was disruptive.

The New York Times printed a letter from Ingrid in April, in which she took issue with a feminist defense of fur-wearing. "Feminists are not struggling for the power to oppress, for the right to be hunters, animal experimenters, fur wearers, and buyers, and butchers," PETA's co-founder wrote. "We are fighting for an ethic that embraces the right to freedom from exploitation, for all. Human chauvinism is not an acceptable replacement for male chauvinism."

In June, Ingrid spoke before 35,000 people who attended PETA's Animal Rights Music Festival, the chronology on the group's website asserted. *The Washington Post* was unimpressed by the event. "It was no surprise to hear various performers enthuse that this was the movement's Woodstock," Kathi Whalen wrote that month. "As a music festival, however, it wasn't spectacular."

Dan Mathews, a PETA employee, organized the event. "We were able to get the grounds of the Washington Monument," he recalled in a brief conversation with this writer. "We had free literature. We had vegan food. It was a really great opportunity to reach out to people in D.C." Ingrid was surprised by the level of attendance. "I remember her being astonished that it was wall-to-wall people, everywhere you looked," Dan said. "We all were astonished, frankly."

Also in June, *The Washington Post* reported that PETA purchased the Aspin Hill Pet Cemetery in Maryland, which a developer had unsuccessfully tried to turn into office space. "Aspin Hill is a wonderful tribute to animals' relationship with people," Ingrid said in the piece by Sue Ann Pressley. "We hope to make it a place of contemplation, but an upbeat place." Former FBI Director J. Edgar Hoover's dogs were buried there. "Built in the 1920s, the cemetery is the final resting spot for a diverse group of about 70,000 creatures," Pressley wrote. "Included are the ashes of more than 15 human masters."

Later that month, Ingrid disputed a poll commissioned by the American Medical Association, which indicated most Americans believed vivisection was necessary for medical progress. "It's hardly an unbiased survey, I must say," she was quoted as saying in an Associated Press article that ran in *The Clovis News-Journal* at the time. Going further, Ingrid accused the AMA of championing "the fight to defeat all legislation on Capitol Hill, no matter how minimal, that would affect the living and dying conditions of animals."

Around that time, Ann Chynoweth—who would go on to become vice president of the Humane Society of the United States' animal cruelty and fighting campaign—started working at PETA, where she met Ingrid. "She intimidated me because I looked up to her so much," Ann said in an interview with this author. "I cared what she thought about me. I just wanted to impress her." Ann described the office culture as free-flowing. "It was very open to trying anything," she recalled. "They really encouraged people who worked there to have their own ideas and to take risks. I always remember Ingrid saying, if you don't make mistakes, you're not doing enough."

After rescuing 200 beavers from a fur farm, PETA's head of investigations, Jeanne Roush, faced a charge of felony theft, according to an Associated Press report, published by *The Kalispell Daily Inter Lake* in November. "The group has publicized the case in its newsletter, prompting a deluge of letters to the *Missoulian* praising

Roush for taking the beavers," the unsigned piece said. "Ingrid Newkirk, national director of the People for the Ethical Treatment of Animals, said the letters are designed to show public sentiment."

Merritt Clifton was curious about what happened to the rescued animals. "Beavers spend all summer building or repairing a winter-proof lodge and stockpiling the food they need to survive the winter," he said in an interview with this writer. "Knowing that these beavers had little more chance of survival in the wild than at the fur farm if they really had been released in the northern Rockies at that time of year, I called PETA to ask what had actually been done with them." Ingrid took Merritt's call herself. "Without admitting in so many words that the beavers had been killed," he said, "Newkirk recited an extended and colorized version of the 1978 Phyllis Wright essay *Why We Must Euthanize*, then seen on the wall of almost every animal shelter."

Also in November, PETA held a party at which famed primatologist Jane Goodall was to be honored, but she boycotted the event because Bubbles—singer Michael Jackson's pet chimpanzee—would be there as well, according to an article in *The Key West Citizen* at the time. Ingrid defended the decision, saying Bubbles was rescued from a research laboratory and served as an ambassador for animal rights. "Seeing how intelligent and social he is, people can see why we have to leave chimps in the dignity of their natural environment," she was quoted as arguing. "He did have a good time at the dinner."

The Washington Post covered the party in a November article. "Then, of course, there was Conchita, a petite, nearly blind 'mixed old dog' belonging to PETA's national director and co-founder, Ingrid Newkirk," wrote journalist Gigi Anders. "She—Conchita—did adhere to swanky specifications and looked entirely elegant in a black satin jacket, complete with a bow tie. Newkirk carried her in her arms for most of the evening."

During Ann's time at PETA, she believed Ingrid was in a romantic relationship with Neal Barnard. "I remember having some documents that I wanted to get to him," Ann recalled in an interview with this writer. "I gave them to her. She said, well, I hope that's not a love note." Of course, Ingrid's comment was meant to be humorous.

In December, an Associated Press report, published by *The Burlington Daily Times*, described how five PETA members and a lawyer entered a holding facility for research animals and refused to leave until the police arrived. "It's clear they are not providing proper veterinary care there," Ingrid said, adding a complaint would be filed with the University of North Carolina at Chapel Hill, which operated the facility.

Liddick stated in his book that, the same year, PETA provided $7,500 to the legal defense of Fran Stephanie Trutt, who attempted to kill the CEO of U.S. Surgical Company with a radio-controlled nail bomb. Writing in the September 1993 edition of *Vegetarian Times*, Erik Marcus seemed to contradict this assertion, saying it was Henry Spira, founder of Animal Rights International, who found Fran a lawyer. "People for the Ethical Treatment of Animals (PETA), the largest animal rights group in the United States, quickly denied any connection to Trutt," he wrote. However, it's possible PETA denied prior connection to Fran while paying a lawyer who Henry found.

According to Bartlett, Fran was a victim of an effort by U.S. Surgical Company to discredit the animal-rights movement. "She was a rather impressionable activist," the movement journalist said in an interview with this writer. "Mary Lou Sapone, who was the agent [provocateur], was looking for someone vulnerable and someone who was not particularly rational. They came across Fran Trutt. She was really into dogs and a little unstable. Anyway, she was persuaded by Mary Lou Sapone to do this."

Ingrid seemed to have pitied Fran. "I remember when the story broke, Ingrid said something to the effect of—that poor, poor woman," Helstosky told this writer. "It was clear that Fran Trutt was not well, emotionally or mentally. It looked awful, like this woman had been convinced to do something that, if she were well, she wouldn't have done. I remember Ingrid's compassion at that time." Helstosky didn't recall any discussion of support for Fran's legal defense.

Also in 1988, according to the chronology on PETA's website, the organization discovered horrific abuses at Biosearch, a laboratory which tested cosmetics and household products. A December piece in *Vegetarian Times* went into further detail. "All in all, PETA accused the lab of more than 100 violations of the federal Animal Welfare Act and Pennsylvania anti-cruelty laws," writer Drew DeSilver stated. "The evidence was presented to Philadelphia District Attorney Ronald Castille; at press time, his office had not decided whether to charge the lab."

5

A NEW HARD LINE

In January of 1989, *Newsday* covered a demonstration outside the headquarters of U.S. Surgical Company, where Ingrid addressed the allegations that Fran had been set up. "Maybe they saw Fran Trutt as a weak link in our chain," PETA's co-founder told the assembled protestors. "But our chain is stronger than the strongest steel. Every day, new links are added."

Ingrid debated a neurosurgeon in February, at the City Club of Cleveland, according to an Associated Press article that ran in *The New Philadelphia Times Reporter*. She contended models and computer simulations should replace animal testing. "The best thing we can do for babies in this country is to turn our priorities to preventative medicine," Ingrid said. "Animals are not our enemies, they are not our toys, they are not our surrogates. They are our fellow inhabitants on Earth."

Ann remembered making a video with Ingrid, around that year, about cats used in research. "It's horrible footage and a tedious process," the future Humane Society of the United States vice president told this writer. "We were putting that together and she said something like, this is all I do." Ann tried to suggest there were worse ways to spend time. "I said, well, Ingrid, think about everybody else in the world—they're watching *Three's Company* or watching TV all day long," Ann stated. "She goes, oh, I would love to do that." This left an impression on Ingrid's subordinate. "She wasn't sanctimonious," Ann said. "I really believed she would rather not be the leader of the movement."

In March, *The Altoona Mirror* reprinted an article that seems to have first appeared in *The Baltimore Evening Sun*, in which Ingrid praised *The Dreaded Comparison,* a book by animal activist Marjorie Spiegel, which compared the treatment of nonhumans to African slaves. "It gets down to the whole package of what animal rights are all about," Ingrid said. Many years later—according to a *New York Sun* report published in August of 2008—Marjorie sued PETA for copyright infringement, apparently arguing the group's use of her concepts discredited the book.

Ingrid talked about expectations for PETA employees in an Associated Press piece, published in March of 1989 by *The Burlington Hawk Eye.* "We have one page of company rules, but it's not like you're joining the army or entering a religious cult," she said. "We have a voluntary ban on smoking and ask employees not to bring in McDonald's burgers." PETA also asked employees not to wear animal products at work. "But we don't run around and inspect people's apparel like the Marines," Ingrid continued. "We hope eventually people will get rid of it, but a lot of people just coming to work here still own something made from an animal."

In April, Ingrid was quoted in *The Panama City News Herald,* discussing World Laboratory Animal Liberation Week. "Civil disobedience is definitely on the ticket across the country," she said. "At a time when there are so many human needs, to be playing around with animals in the basements of universities seems not only cruel to animals but wasteful of dollars."

Civil disobedience was indeed on the ticket, as shown by a United Press International report, published in *The Marshall Chronicle.* "Hundreds of activists protesting experiments on animals halted traffic outside the National Institutes of Health Monday and at least 21 were arrested when the crowd charged a building and broke down a door," the unsigned piece stated. "[Ingrid] said activists chose to demonstrate at NIH—a federal agency that is the nation's leading biomedical research facility—because it is the largest funder of animal experimenters in the world."

In May, Ingrid dismissed any positive impact that vivisection might have in a personal manner. "It's immoral even if it's essential," she told Specter, who was writing for *The Washington Post* at the time. "You just cannot justify the torture and destruction of innocent animals. If my father had a heart attack it would give me no solace at all to know his treatment was first tried on a dog."

Ingrid argued vivisection was unhelpful for AIDS research, *The Janesville Sunday Gazette* reported in a July article. "AZT—the drug approved for the treatment of people infected with the HIV virus— was discovered in vitro 15 years ago, not from any research done on an animal, said Ingrid Newkirk," according to reporter Carla McCann. "AIDS only has been isolated in the human population, not in chipmunks, cats or bears. Why researchers continue to inject the virus in animals that fail to develop true cases of the disease is a mystery, Newkirk said."

When the Agriculture Department proposed new regulations on animal research, Ingrid brushed off claims by the testing industry that the changes would be too expensive to implement. "We have never seen such a concentrated, concerted effort by those who use animals, those who supply animals, [and] others involved in the experimentation community to protect every penny of their livelihood," she was quoted as saying in a piece published by *The Washington Post* in July.

Ingrid vented her own frustration, pointing out rodents—the most commonly used research animals—weren't covered in the proposed rules. "All animals who are used must be covered," she told Judith Havemann, author of *The Washington Post* article. "It doesn't matter to the animals whether their blood is warm or cold, whether they are big or small, ugly or attractive. They all are entitled to minimal protection."

PETA delivered two tons of manure to the headquarters of Ringling Brothers and Barnum & Bailey Circus, along with a sign that read 'Animal Cruelty Stinks.' Ingrid explained the rationale behind the protest in an Associated Press brief that ran in *The Cumberland Sunday Times-News* that month. "Ringling Brothers keeps mistreating their animals," she said. "They are really the worst of all the circuses."

According to a July article in *The Washington Post*, two PETA leaders—Alex Pacheco and Carol Burnett—were indicted on charges of assaulting a police officer during the April protest at NIH. While the Maryland U.S. attorney said the felony charges were intended to mark a new hard line against animal activists, Ingrid said the effort would only inspire more protest. "It's not going to work," she told reporter Paul W. Valentine. "It's going to backfire." Ultimately the accused PETA leaders were acquitted, according to a December follow-up in the same newspaper.

In August, *The Clearfield Progress* published an Associated Press article that described how the remains of dogs and cats were rendered into substances used in a host of products. Ingrid appeared to reluctantly approve of this. "You're grateful if anyone will come and take the bodies away," she was quoted as saying. "They don't keep well. You must put them in giant freezers. It's hideous. A lousy, lousy situation."

Later that month, *The Washington Post* ran a preview of the Montgomery County Agricultural Fair, where PETA had established a presence in the past. "PETA bid successfully last year on five sheep, now residents of the [Aspin Hill] sanctuary," reporter Claudia Levy wrote. "Several crying children at the auction begged PETA representatives to buy their animals, said Ingrid Newkirk, director of the organization." Activists generally discourage such seemingly merciful purchases as they encourage further exploitation.

Near the end of August, *The New York Times* reported on the killing of one captive orca by another at SeaWorld. "These kinds of incidents draw our attention in the ghastliest way possible to the inappropriateness of the animals' living conditions," Ingrid said. "It's wrong that the people who run these enterprises are really preying on people's interest and attraction to these rather exotic animals." She continued, blaming attendees for "unwittingly paying for more and more captures, more disruption of pods and family life, more loneliness and stress for the whales."

Ingrid wrote a message to *The Washington Post,* which was printed in November, slamming the newspaper for publicizing research based on animal testing. "Who was suffering the most from impaired cognitive biorhythms?" Ingrid asked. "The experimenters who strapped seven rhesus monkeys into uncomfortable restraint devices and made them pull levers in response to blinking lights for eight hours to 'study jet lag?' Or you who, by reporting such rot, encourage the proliferation of crude but expensive studies that could clearly be carried out more effectively by humans who voluntarily fly to Paris or Rome?"

Later that month, in a *New York Times* profile of Henry Spira, Ingrid accused the founder of Animal Rights International of being too willing to compromise. "He is hobnobbing in the halls with our enemy," she said. "Six or seven years ago, we had a lot in common. Everything he did then was putting gravel down for other people to pave roads, which was crucial. But I think Henry was deceived by the industry response. Henry was unable to cut himself loose from the mire of having become an industry mediator."

In December, *The Walla Walla Union-Bulletin* published an Associated Press piece, in which Ingrid previewed PETA's Christmas-themed activism. Demonstrators dressed as elves would hand out naughty and nice lists—that highlighted products that were tested on animals or used animal products, and those that didn't—in 100 cities. "Many people don't realize how their shopping choices affect the welfare of animals," Ingrid said in the unsigned article. "We want peace and goodwill for all during this holiday season, including the 14 million animals who die needlessly in product tests every year."

Later that month, Ingrid defended anti-hunting activists with a column printed by *The Gettysburg Times*. "While hunters go out to obtain some (sexual?) gratification and bag some flesh (at a greater cost per pound, on average, than store-bought meat), concerned animal protectionists are there to bear witness and to defend the defenseless," she wrote. "Hunt sabotage is not about preventing the pleasure of hunters, but rather about protecting the lives of animals and saving them from the disruption and fear inherent in the hunt." Ingrid went on, outlining the ways in which wild-life management programs—nominally intended to control animal populations—create a 'surplus' of nonhumans, at significant public expense, specifically for hunters to kill.

Also in 1989, PETA convinced many large companies to stop testing on animals, according to the chronology on the organization's website. These companies included Avon, Benetton, Mary Kay, Amway, Kenner, Mattel, and Hasbro. Swarthmore College's Global Nonviolent Action Database gave a sense of the campaigning involved: "PETA members went door-to-door to distribute three million door-hangers on homes that read 'Avon Killing,' a play on the cosmetic company's advertising." Unfortunately, the changes were short-lived. "Many of these companies have started testing on animals again to sell their products in China," PETA's chronology noted.

Despite these corporate reversals, Paul Shapiro, founder of Compassion Over Killing, didn't believe PETA should have focused on legislative action. "You can't have the cake and eat it too," he told this writer. "You can't engage in these tactics that made people think—I don't want to talk to them—and then also try to influence lawmakers." Further, Paul argued PETA's approach was valuable. "Public policy and corporate policy are two sides of the same coin," he said. "They both help drive each other."

At the time of the interview, Paul was vice president of farm animal protection at the Humane Society of the United States, before leaving the organization under a cloud of sexual misconduct allegations. "We're pursuing a bill in Congress, right now, for example, that would not only ban the testing of cosmetics on animals but also would ban the sale of cosmetics tested on animals in the United States," he said to this writer. "That would never have been possible if these companies had never adopted these policies in the first place. PETA had a lot of success."

In February of 1990, *USA Today* covered debates taking place at veterinary schools across the country, about the use of healthy animals for training and other matters. Ingrid expressed frustration at the pace of reform. "There's a lot of change to be made yet," she told journalists, Don Knorr and Dennis Kelly. "These are baby steps being taken." Among several suggestions, PETA's co-founder said veterinary schools should establish wildlife clinics, so students could work with nonhumans in need of assistance.

Ingrid discussed speciesism in an article published by *The Chicago Daily Herald* later that month. "It's the human hand of tyranny," she told journalist Cheryl Horst. "We have been truly obnoxious children on the face of the earth. We've been extremely overbearing and we have denied animals their basic needs to breed, to be free. If we're really at the top, the most important thing is to be number one in compassion."

The Chicago Daily Herald ran a piece in March, which included, among other things, Ingrid imagining a future without pets. "You don't have to own squirrels and starlings to get enjoyment from them," she said to Horst, adding that because domestication would prevent companion animals from surviving in the wild, they should be gradually phased out. "One day, we would like an end to pet shops and the breeding of animals."

Later that month—in a *Washington Post* article about a drug capable of reducing spinal-injury damage—Ingrid took a practical approach to treatments developed using animal testing. "I think you can't turn back the clock and say, 'I wish it had been done some other way,'" she told reporter Susan Okle. "If it is truly useful, the fact that they used animals somewhere along the way is an unfortunate reality."

In a piece that ran in *The Los Angeles Times* in April, Ingrid spoke about PETA's lawsuit against a magazine writer who alleged PETA staged photographs in the Silver Spring monkey case and engaged in financial improprieties. "I expect backlash, but I didn't expect it to be [so] dirty," Ingrid said. "I didn't expect outright lies." The magazine writer had previously been paid to make nearly twenty speeches in front of scientific groups about animal rights.

On the same day, *The Orlando Sentinel* printed a story, in which Frederick K. Goodwin—head of the Alcohol, Drug Abuse and Mental Health Administration—argued animal activists were obstructing medical progress. Ingrid responded in fiery fashion. "The agency he (Goodwin) heads up is busy putting money into making pigs alcoholics and into making monkeys cocaine addicts when there are people out there who can't get into programs for addiction," PETA's co-founder said. "There are people out there who could have these conditions prevented if he spent his time in the workplaces and in the schools teaching people that you can prevent some of these problems, you can early-detect some of these problems and that you can provide therapy for some of these problems."

Ingrid opposed a bill that would make rescuing animals from farms and laboratories a federal crime, punishable by three years in prison and a $10,000 fine, according to an Associated Press article published in May by *The Big Spring Herald*. "Ingrid Newkirk, national director of People for the Ethical Treatment of Animals, urged lawmakers instead to create an adequate way to review allegations of animal abuse," the unsigned article stated.

On the eve of the historic March for Animals, the Health and Human Services Secretary referred to animal advocates as terrorists, the Associated Press reported in a June piece published by *The Kalispell Daily Inter-Lake*. Ingrid, of course, took exception to this. She called the official's comment "appalling," and said it was "an attempt to gloss over all the exposés of terrible cruelties, fraud and unnecessary use of animals."

In July, Ingrid again bashed the bill meant to stamp out the ALF, saying it would violate the First Amendment, seal animal-welfare records, and discourage whistleblowers—according to an Associated Press article published in *The Big Spring Herald* that month. She endorsed alternate legislation, which would allow people to file lawsuits on animals' behalf. Such a law would "eliminate any excuse for anyone claiming that an illegal action was the only way to stop violations of animal care regulations," Ingrid said.

That year, PETA exposed animal abuse by a Las Vegas showman, prompting his wildlife permit to be suspended and the end of his act, the chronology on the organization's website asserted. An August article in *The Los Angeles Times* described the abuse. "A video camera hidden backstage at the Stardust hotel-casino recorded headliner Bobby Berosini hitting his orangutans across the back with a rod while handlers held the apes' hands," journalist Kevin Roderick wrote. "The treatment is repeated on tape several nights, moments before Berosini and his apes take the stage for their act of gags and tricks during the Lido de Paris floor show."

In September, *The New York Times* covered PETA's 10th Anniversary Humanitarian Awards Gala. There were several celebrities in attendance, including "Tom Scholz, songwriter and guitarist with the rock band Boston; Elliot Gould, the veteran actor; K.D. Lang, the Canadian country singer and anti-meat spokeswoman, and Chrissie Hynde of The Pretenders," reporter Olwen Woodier wrote. Ingrid attempted to create a jovial atmosphere. "Let's try and put the suffering of animals out of our minds for one night and have fun," she was quoted as saying to those assembled.

Ingrid discussed PETA's Dump L'Oréal and Dump Gillette efforts in an interview with Knight Ridder Newspapers, published by *The Orange County Register* in November. "This campaign is a challenge because we're taking on two huge companies at the same time," she said. "Other companies have stopped testing, but these two have decided to fight it out. They think they are too big, that we can't get consumers to take products back."

That year, Karen Davis launched United Poultry Concerns, which Ingrid supported wholeheartedly. "There were people—leaders, semi-leaders in the movement—in the late 1980s, who, when I talked to them about starting an organization that would focus on chickens and turkeys, said to me, you'll never make that work," Karen told this writer, noting Ingrid wasn't such a person. "She was one of those who said, yeah, great idea; do it. She gave us the motto that we still use and have on buttons and elsewhere: Stick Up for Chickens."

6

THE ANIMAL
MOVEMENT'S FOREMOST
ENFANT TERRIBLE

In 1991, the U.S. Supreme Court allowed two of the remaining Silver Spring monkeys to be put to death, over PETA's objections, according to an April article published in *The Los Angeles Times*. "Animal rights groups tried to stop the euthanasia in federal courts," the unsigned report stated. "They won a temporary victory Wednesday when Justice Anthony M. Kennedy issued a temporary restraining order. Kennedy joined seven other justices on Friday, however, in lifting that order. Justice Antonin Scalia did not participate."

Also in April, *The Washington Post* reported PETA put to death 18 rabbits and 14 roosters, for whom the organization could not find homes. Ingrid said the animals were killed due to space constraints at the sanctuary PETA established at Aspin Hill. She denied this was hypocritical, following her group's attempt to save the Silver Spring monkeys. "We will not overcrowd our animals," Ingrid said. "We really didn't have anything else to do. And so, euthanasia was carried out with a great deal of concern."

In the same article, Ingrid told *The Washington Post* that PETA opposed killing the Silver Spring monkeys because the organization didn't believe researchers' claims that the animals' health had deteriorated. "Euthanasia means mercy killing," she said. "What we are opposed to is the unnecessary slaughter of animals for frivolous reasons. If they [the monkeys] need euthanasia, we have always said we would go along with that." The health of the rabbits and roosters does not appear to have been in question.

Ingrid further defended PETA's decisions at the Aspin Hill sanctuary in a letter to *The Anderson Herald Bulletin*, published in August. "There is a lot of difference between euthanasia and the wanton destruction of life for political and public relations reasons," she wrote, suggesting the latter was what researchers involved in the Silver Spring monkey case had engaged in. "Because there are not enough homes for all the abused animals who need them, PETA chooses to work at the roots, stopping the flow of animals born or captured only to be kept under miserable conditions and then be shot, have their throats slit, or worse."

After disrupting an annual pigeon shoot, Ingrid and other activists were arrested—according to an Associated Press report, which *The Wayne Independent* ran in September. Ingrid, having refused to post bail, was quoted discussing conditions at Schuylkill County Prison. "What we're facing here is uncomfortable and it's unpleasant, but it's nothing compared to what the animals must go through," she said, remaining on message. "We'll stay here as long as we have to."

Around that time, Jonathan Balcombe, who would go on to write the bestselling book *What a Fish Knows*, joined PETA as a researcher. "[The office was] generally a very positive, humming place," he recalled, in an interview with this writer. "People were really nice. I liked my colleagues by and large. There was an excited energy there." Jonathan added the workforce seemed to be predominantly made up of young women. "I don't remember cubicles," he said. "It was a dog-friendly office."

Ingrid's organization held monthly, all-staff meetings. "There were several people who would be called on to just update on what they'd done," Jonathan said to this writer. "That would be PR people [and] media people. Ingrid would kind of direct the meetings." Strategy didn't seem to be up for debate in these gatherings. "I never had the sense it was fully an autocracy," he said when asked about this. "But it was a bit autocratic."

Jonathan typically saw Ingrid about once or twice a week. "I don't mean to give the impression that Ingrid was aloof or deliberately out of view," he told this writer. "I think a lot of it was that she was on the go—on the road, traveling a great deal. She probably still is. She was always in demand to speak, to be interviewed in the media, and, of course, there were activism things that she was doing." Jonathan estimated that in the 16 months he worked at PETA, he spoke one-on-one with Ingrid a dozen times or fewer.

Still, Jonathan experienced Ingrid's temper. "She was quite a mercurial person to work for," he said, in an interview with this writer. "To her credit, she praised me. There were times—more than once—when I came into my office, and my phone was beeping." There would be a message from Ingrid, congratulating him on a letter he'd written to the editor of a newspaper. "The flip-side was, I mean, I got thrashed once verbally," Jonathan said. "She was not happy with what I'd done or what I was doing. She was quite direct, harsh and not at all nice."

This incident contributed to Jonathan's decision to leave PETA. "It was like she was in a bad mood and she was taking it out on me," he told this writer. "I'm not the kind of person to slack off or to rub people the wrong way. And I'm pretty sensitive. I have somewhat thin skin. So that really jarred me. It was probably the beginning of my plan to look elsewhere and find other work."

In *I Am an Animal*, the 2007 HBO documentary, Ingrid traced her impatience to Noel Ward. "My father had great anger that would well up from inside him," PETA's co-founder said. "He had a fierce temper. I work to not have it, but there are occasions when I really have almost done physical damage to people."

In 1992, PETA contributed $42,000 to the legal defense of ALF member Rod Coronado, the Southern Poverty Law Center asserted in a timeline posted to its website about animal-rights and environmental radicalism. Liddick provided a slightly higher figure in his book—$45,200—and claimed PETA also sent $25,000 to Rod's father. (Attempts to interview Rod for this book were unsuccessful.)

Josh Harper spoke highly of the contribution. "PETA suffered for it greatly," he told this writer. "That donation remains controversial to this day. You can go onto websites—mostly the Center for Consumer Freedom and its various AstroTurf entities—where that donation still gets brought up. So I admire [Ingrid] for doing that. I'm glad that she had the sort of relationship with Rod that allowed him to get that type of support." According to Josh, Rod and PETA's co-founder were personal friends.

That year, Ingrid's book, *Free the Animals*—which claimed to tell the true story of the North American Animal Liberation Front—was published. In the text, Ingrid described a meeting between a pseudonymous activist and Ronnie Lee, founder of the ALF, about establishing the underground group in the United States. Speaking with this writer, Ronnie said the meeting was a complete fabrication. "There was never an instance," he said, "where I made someone fool around and lift up their clothes, so I could see if there was a listening device." Similarly, Ronnie didn't send the activist to an ALF training camp, because as far as he knew, the camp didn't exist.

However, Ronnie remembered meeting PETA's co-founder in the late 1970s or early 1980s, when Ingrid came to visit the British Union for the Abolition of Vivisection. "The BUAV allowed me to use a desk in their offices," he told this writer. "My recollection is that she came into the BUAV just to see people in general, and I was there." Ronnie believed it was possible they went to a pub, which was the setting for Ingrid's account of a meeting between him and the pseudonymous activist. "Quite often, several of us would go to a local pub, sit around and have a chat," he said. "It was a place that used to do some food that was suitable for vegans."

Ronnie suspected Ingrid had fictionalized her own meeting with him, adding elements of espionage for dramatic effect. "I always wondered whether that was her," he said to this writer. "Basically, I'd met Ingrid. We'd had a conversation. Then she turned that into the elaborate story in the book, and used another character in her place." Ronnie acknowledged the pseudonymous activist might have been real and had misled Ingrid. "If someone told Ingrid this, Ingrid wouldn't have known it was untrue," he said.

The Los Angeles Times published a story in January of 1992, about the Rose Parade, which PETA protested due to the inclusion of a General Motors float. The car company engaged in animal research. "Ingrid Newkirk, the organization's national director, leaped out of the crowd wearing a pink bunny suit and was joined by two men in pig and rat costumes," journalists Frank Clifford and Henry Weinstein wrote. "The protestors were quickly corralled by deputies and hauled away to a waiting squad car." Animal activists were overshadowed by Native American groups demonstrating against the parade's grand marshal, a descendant of Christopher Columbus, chosen to celebrate his ancestor's expedition to the New World.

In February, PETA launched one of its most iconic campaigns, according to the organization's chronology. The Associated Press covered the stunt, in a piece The Los Angeles Times made available on its website. "Two Americans protested the fur business Tuesday by stripping down to their underwear and marching through a crowded shopping district carrying a banner reading, 'We'd Rather Go Naked Than Wear Fur,'" the unsigned article stated. "Ignoring the chilly 46-degree weather, Dan Mathews and Julia Sloane of the Washington-based People for the Ethical Treatment of Animals walked for an hour outside Sunshine 60, Japan's tallest building."

In an interview posted to her website, Carol Adams—author of *The Sexual Politics of Meat*—summarized her criticism of the campaign. "[It] gives lots of animal rights activists another way to harass women," she said. "That's my first objection. My second objection is that the 'I'd rather go naked than wear fur' campaign just accepts the cultural construction of women's bodies as commodities. And thirdly, I think that subliminally what this campaign says is you can still have objects in your life, they just can't be animals. You can still have women objects."

Karen Davis was troubled by PETA's increasing reliance on nudity, not because it degraded women, but because it degraded animals. "What I'm not okay with is using frivolity, pornography or semi-pornography, and women using their sexuality to bring attention to the plight of suffering, abused animals," she told this writer. "It's not that I disagree with the right of women to use their bodies as they please, although I don't care for that kind of thing myself. But I think it's demeaning to the animals and their misery."

In March, *The Eau Claire Leader-Telegram* published an Associated Press article about the Wisconsin Animal Rights Convention. Ingrid spoke at the event, arguing for moral consistency. "We have anti-cruelty-to-animals laws in this country, but if we think cruelty to animals is wrong, then we can't look only to cruelty to 'cute' animals or to those that live in our homes," she was quoted as saying. "We were primitive once. We gnawed on raw flesh and wore only animal skins. But it is 1992 now, and we are supposed to be thinking, caring, compassionate animals."

Later that month, *The Los Angeles Times* ran a long profile of Ingrid, that referenced, among other things, her plan to dress up as a condom to protest prophylactic companies testing on animals, PETA throwing pies at opponents, and one of the group's advertisements, which compared the meat industry to Jeffrey Dahmer. Ingrid defended such tactics. "Say something sensible without a gimmick, and it will be ignored," she told writer Howard Rosenberg. "So you're reduced—and that's what it is—to doing something often absurd."

Still, Rosenberg made clear Ingrid suffered for her role as the animal movement's foremost enfant terrible. "Newkirk gets hate mail," he wrote in *The Los Angeles Times* piece. "A hunter warned her to watch out for a stray bullet, cruel jokesters mail her the heads of animals, at Christmas a sicko sent her a brightly wrapped box containing a skinned cat. Her car has been shot at in the PETA parking lot, and she won't reveal where she lives for fear of placing herself and others in jeopardy."

Rosenberg's article also showed PETA alienating would-be allies—like the group's former lawyer, Gary Francione, who would go on to become an influential author of animal-rights philosophy. "They were nice people once, and I worked with them for a long time," Gary said. "But as they got bigger and got more money, the star-demigod syndrome took over, and Ingrid and Alex started believing they were the only voices of animal rights." (Attempts to interview Gary for this book were unsuccessful.)

Near the end of March, in a *Washington Post* article, Ingrid was quoted bashing the founder of Putting People First, a group dedicated to preserving animal exploitation. She described the reactionary, who she occasionally debated, as "sort of Neanderthal . . . It's sad, in a way, when you think that people have expanded their ethical boundaries . . . and then you run into this mentality, which is full of venom and nastiness, a very selfish perspective: money money money, me me me me me."

In May, *The Washington Post* ran a letter from Ingrid, complaining about World Day for Animals in Laboratories' lack of coverage. "Your paper devoted significant space to laud a revolting series of experiments in which captured octopuses are electro-shocked," she wrote, adding the piece's author suggested PETA members were terrorists when communicating with the organization. "Is this one-sidedness so pervasive that your paper was comfortable omitting all mention of activities . . . in commemoration of the tens of millions of animals, from octopuses to chimpanzees, who suffer and are killed each year in our nation's laboratories?

The Indiana Gazette published an Associated Press article in July, in which Ingrid discussed the 1992 protest of the aforementioned pigeon shoot. "This year we want to shut it down," she said, noting hundreds of more demonstrators planned to attend the event. Speaking at the same news conference, another PETA activist recounted the poor conditions at Schuylkill County Prison. Apparently, ten protestors had recently sued the local government for their treatment the prior year.

While promoting *Free the Animals*, Ingrid expressed confidence the ALF wouldn't accidentally harm someone, according to an August piece in *The Philadelphia Daily News*. "I don't believe there is any chance," she told journalist Kathleen Shea. "It's not that they think, 'Oooooh, people have gone home for the night. Let's raze this building.' They enter these facilities, they go through them from every crack to every corner and they make sure there's nobody in them. I think the first thing that will go wrong is somebody will shoot one of them."

Ingrid was quoted, in a September column published by *The Gettysburg Times*, explaining her controversial views on sheltering. "I would rather lose sleep at night knowing that I sent a dog to heaven, or let a dog drift away to nothingness, than know that I am responsible for allowing him to spend the next six years on a ten-foot piece of chain beside the trash can," she said, before arguing against no-kill shelters. "[Those facilities] either turn their backs on many of the truly needy by being discretionary, or they quietly give the animals they cannot place to another shelter for euthanasia."

Peter Singer spoke highly of Ingrid's stance. "I think she's courageous for defending it," he told this writer. "There are cases where an animal is suffering, or where the prospect of an animal having a good future is low, or simply where the burden of caring for the animals in a way that would give them a good future is very high and would prevent you doing other things that would more reduce suffering. So I think that humanely ending the life of an animal in those circumstances is defensible and compatible with opposition to speciesism."

At that year's pigeon shoot, Ingrid was arrested again, according to an Associated Press report *The Titusville Herald* ran in September. "Newkirk, one of the imprisoned animal-rights activists, said inmates were left without potable water and proper sanitation facilities after a water-main break," the unsigned article stated. "Three women contracted giardiasis, a painful intestinal ailment caused by a water-borne parasite, she said. Ms. Newkirk said a doctor visited the ill inmates but did not have any kind of medication to help them. She said the prison is cold, but that inmates must keep their windows open to counter the stench caused by backed-up toilets and sinks."

In October, *The Fort Lauderdale Sun-Sentinel* printed the results of an audit, which showed the Animal, Plant and Health Inspection Service was dramatically understaffed. Ingrid was unsurprised. "We live in hope that things will get better, but APHIS' record is one of the worst in government," PETA's co-founder told reporter Kim Margolis. "Their mandate now seems to be to protect business."

An Associated Press piece, published later that month by *The Burlington Hawk Eye*, revealed PETA's founders were ensnared in a probe of the ALF. "Pacheco said he and Ingrid Newkirk, PETA national director, have been subpoenaed by the Michigan grand jury to provide handwriting samples, fingerprints, and photos of themselves," reporter Jennifer Dixon wrote. "Pacheco said he believes he is a target of the investigation." In the same article, industry representatives suggested the probe showed authorities' new seriousness, following the passage of the Animal Enterprise Protection Act.

Stallwood wrote in his autobiography that he left PETA in 1992. "For reasons I've never quite fathomed, the relationship between Alex and Ingrid and me changed," Stallwood wrote, clarifying that he never received negative feedback about his work. "I found myself being excluded from key decisions. Important information was withheld from me, and I was slowly shut out of the organization. Although she never stated explicitly, Ingrid made clear to me that she wanted me to leave."

Perhaps Ingrid sensed Stallwood was starting to have misgivings about PETA's direction. "Inexorably, we began to make decisions about actions whose sole purpose was to get coverage,'" he wrote in his autobiography, adding he and Ingrid referred to themselves as media whores. "We believed that all coverage was worthwhile, even if it meant framing PETA and animal rights in a negative light, and even if it meant our ads were banned because they were too controversial. In fact, we fell in love with controversy. Outrage became our friend."

Bartlett seemed to believe Ingrid had no choice but to pursue sensational tactics. "The media makes it necessary," the movement journalist argued in an interview with this writer. "You can't go to them and say—I have this very serious issue and I'd like to present it in its essential form. No, they want sex, scandal or celebrity."

7

VIOLATION OF THE FEMININE

A significant number of activists protested the Los Angeles Auto Show due to General Motors' use of animals in product testing, United Press International reported in a brief article, that ran in *European Stars and Stripes* in January of 1993. "Newkirk said members of her group would be present at every GM stockholders' meeting, golf tournament and car show until GM stops using animals in tests," the unsigned piece stated. The company stopped testing on animals that year, according to the chronology on PETA's website.

Later that month, *Newsday* reported on a possible sign that the relationship between PETA and the government was thawing. "We've learned from Dan Mathews of People for the Ethical Treatment of Animals that for the first time, the organization's national director, Ingrid Newkirk, was invited in by members of Clinton's transition team last week to discuss the issues," journalists Anthony Scaduto, Doug Vaughan and Linda Stasi wrote. "This is a big leap for animal-rights folk because, under Bush, Newkirk's only contact with the government was her ever-growing FBI file."

In March, *Newsday* covered an anti-fur demonstration, that featured a bit of street theater. "Animal-rights activists staged a mock funeral yesterday in front of a Fifth Avenue fur salon to protest the fur trade and celebrate what they say is the inevitable death of the industry," reporter Julio Laboy wrote. "Protesters constructed a graveyard on the concrete with ten cardboard tombstones representing several furriers who have recently gone out of business." Ingrid was there. "Fur means condemning animals to suffocation, anal electrocution, and poisoning," PETA's co-founder said. "What are we, cave people? There is no excuse for fur."

Ingrid traveled to Israel—on a trip planned to coincide with the opening of the Tel Aviv SPCA shelter—according to a June piece in *The Jerusalem Post*. "It's been a very short visit but I have seen a lot," she told journalist Liat Collins. "I've seen a tremendous number of strays, all those thin cats you can see on the streets here." PETA's co-founder pushed for neutering and an end to the use of strychnine poison to kill unwanted animals.

In the wake of bomb scares at vivisectors' homes, a county council began considering legislation prohibiting activists from protesting in residential neighborhoods, *The Washington Post* asserted in a July article. Ingrid appeared to oppose the measure. "A person that commits atrocities shouldn't be able to get off work at the end of the day and be insulated beyond the Constitution," she told reporter Charles Babington.

In August, Ingrid wrote a column for *The Washington Post*, in which she used the success of a children's film to decry exploitation of wild animals in entertainment. "The summer movie *Free Willy* has people talking again about placing a moratorium on seizing whales and other marine mammals from their ocean homes, often for no more compelling a reason than to see them perform tricks in amusement park aquariums," Ingrid observed. "Of course, elephants, the 'whales of the land,' don't have much more of a life under the Big Top than the 'Willies' do in their tanks."

Ingrid wrote a September column for *Newsday*, defending a New York City ferret ban. "The health department is right, but for the wrong reason," PETA's co-founder argued. "If you want to share your life with an animal, there's no need to pay the pet-shop pimps and other flesh traders to tailor-make you a furry this or a red-feathered that —or to seize a weird animal from his or her jungle, forest or ocean home. At every animal shelter there are wonderful, intelligent, needy dogs and cats, pacing back and forth on death row, hoping a kind human will come by, take them home and love them."

In October, The Guardian ran a story about Ingrid's efforts to expand her organization's reach. "When she opens PETA's European headquarters in London next month, Newkirk will already have released a video, presented by Sir John Gielgud, attacking the consumption of pate de foie gras," journalist Nick Rosen wrote. "She will simultaneously launch *Animal Times*, a pan-European monthly, supported by advertising, and no doubt, a hefty grant from PETA in the US, which has an annual budget of about $10 million."

Ingrid toured the Wright State University laboratory, according to a piece published later that month by *The Dayton Daily News*. "Corridors is mostly what I saw," she told reporter Jim Bland. "They had all of the areas in which they work on animals shielded from me by blinds or paper over the window. I asked to be allowed to film or tape as I went through, and they denied that." A school representative claimed the rooms were shielded because researchers were conducting experiments involving different kinds of light.

That year, Matt Ball, co-founder of Vegan Outreach, invited Ingrid to speak at the University of Illinois at Urbana-Champaign. "She gave two talks and she did a number of radio interviews," he told this author. "It was exhausting just to watch her. I was like, I should cut her off; I should say, one more question. But she was just raring to go." Ingrid met with animal activists after her scheduled events. "She still seemed very energized," Matt said. "She didn't seem drained by it at all."

Matt had recently read *Free the Animals*, which left him deeply inspired by the Animal Liberation Front. "I thought that what I was doing was kind of wimpy—it wasn't as hardcore as what the situation called for," he said in an interview with this writer. "So I told her that her book made me wonder if I should be doing 'parties,' which was the code phrase for it in the book. She said, no, no, you should definitely be doing what you're doing."

Ingrid was arrested in London for her participation in PETA's Rather Go Naked Than Wear Fur campaign, according to an Associated Press report, which *The Port Arthur News* ran in December. "Three animal rights activists sent their message to Christmas shoppers Tuesday by parading naked except for Santa hats, gloves, and an anti-fur banner," the unsigned piece stated. "The protestors, two of them American, attracted a large crowd of police, news photographers and gawkers on Regent Street in a busy Christmas shopping area."

Jane Velez-Mitchell, a former CNN anchor who now runs the activist website Jane Unchained, brushed off non-vegan criticism of PETA's Rather Go Naked Campaign. "What I think is the ultimate violation of the feminine is factory farming," she said in an interview with this writer, noting animals endured unwanted sexual penetration in the process. "Maybe feminists—instead of attacking Ingrid Newkirk and women taking desperate measures to wake up a populace that is hellbent on remaining in denial— should focus their attention on their behavior."

Designer Calvin Klein announced he would no longer make clothes using fur, *The New York Times* said in an article published in February of 1994. "His statement to the press yesterday seemed less tied to [the expiration of licensing agreements] than to the invasion of Mr. Klein's offices on Jan. 25 by People for Ethical Treatment of Animals," journalist Amy M. Spindler wrote. "Mr. Klein seemed to want to avoid being seen as under the group's influence, which is considerable in the fashion world." Regardless, the chronology on PETA's website said he was the first major fashion designer to make such a decision.

Around that year, Ingrid debated Adams. "Feminists for Animal Rights asked Ingrid and me to have a conversation about the naked campaigns," Adams recalled in an interview with this writer. "It was going to be carried in the Feminists for Animal Rights newsletter. So we set a time to do that. Ingrid launched into her defense first— they were taping it—and then I responded. But her assistant failed to turn the tape over. So all my responses were lost."

Ingrid was too busy to record the debate again. "I didn't feel a conversation was a conversation if we both weren't on it," Adams told this author. "In addition, when she was defending the naked campaign, she sort of defended pornography and said, what's wrong with men—I can't remember how she said it—jerking off to calendars in their garage? At that point, I thought that I respected her enough that I didn't want the conversation to be published because I knew that she'd completely lose a lot of feminist support."

Speaking to *The Los Angeles Times*, in an article from March of 1994, Ingrid was pleased to learn of a sea lion's escape from a training exercise clearing dummy mines. "Good for him," she said to reporter Patrick McCartney. "The Navy declared war on marine mammals a long time ago. It's too bad the Geneva Convention doesn't extend to sea lions."

Ingrid protested the Grand National in an April letter printed by *The London Times*. "Horse racing's best-known event is also its most bloody," she wrote. "We understand that 26 horses have been killed on the course in the Grand National's 155-year history: one dead horse for every four races, without taking account of the scores of horses injured during the race that have ultimately had to be 'put down,' or the many others that are injured on courses throughout Britain every week."

In a May piece, that ran in *The Los Angeles Times*, Ingrid argued the American Humane Association wasn't capable of monitoring Hollywood. "The AHA would admit that certainly, they aren't usually (on sets)," she said. "It's unrealistic and impossible, given all the films in which animals are used, for them to be present for even the tiniest percentage of them." Ingrid continued, adding nonhuman trainers could be ignorant and brutal. "We learned that many don't know what the federal Animal Welfare Act requires of them," she said, "and their feelings are that animals are no more than props that are quite expendable."

Following a rash of escapes by circus elephants, in which the animals sometimes maimed their captors, Ingrid recalled her interaction with a captive elephant named Rani, apparently trying to put a face on the issue. "She stood outside the Ashoka Hotel in New Delhi, India, from sunrise to late at night, waiting to be prodded into action whenever a tourist fancied a ride," Ingrid wrote in a column published by *The Panama City News Herald* in August. "When I first saw Rani, I couldn't have been much taller than her knee, but she was extremely gentle."

Ingrid said it wasn't until later she appreciated the stunted lives endured by captive animals like Rani, who were literally beaten into submission. PETA's co-founder concluded her piece in *The Panama City News Herald*, by looping back to the recent elephant escapes, which resulted in both human and nonhuman bloodshed. "Perhaps the tragedies of this month will be lesson enough for us to demand that our legislators ban captive animal performances and to redirect our children's attention to other entertainments that avoid exploitation," Ingrid wrote.

In December, *The New York Times* printed a story, in which Ingrid pushed back against claims the anti-fur movement was fueled by misogyny. "Whoever is wearing fur hears from people who are appalled by the pain and suffering and death," PETA's co-founder told reporter Julia Szabo. "Women should not be considered so frail that we have to be insulated from criticism. If we are doing something that's appalling, it doesn't matter what gender, what race, what age, what anything we are—cruelty is cruelty."

In 1995, PETA convinced several oil companies to place covers on their exhaust stacks, which had been killing millions of birds and bats, according to the chronology on the group's website. In his book, *Voices from the Underground*, Michael Tobias described the campaigning involved. "The animal-rights organization held rallies in front of Mobil's offices in Houston, as well as before eleven other oil giants," Tobias wrote, adding the fix was quite cheap. "The oil industry did what it needed to get the activists off its back: it decided to use the caps, simple cone-shaped devices which cost them an average of 14 dollars each."

Ingrid praised a researcher who was teaching chimpanzees American Sign Language, according to a January piece in *The Baltimore Sun*. "If [Roger Fouts] can help people understand how to communicate, one primate to another, then bravo," she told reporter Tina Kelley. "We need to stop being so arrogant and listen to what all the other animals have to say, even if they're compelled to try to communicate with us in our own language, which is in itself an indictment of our lack of understanding."

After a chinchilla breeder relocated his operation out of the country—as part of a settlement to avoid an animal cruelty charge—Ingrid claimed the fur industry pushed authorities to dismiss the case. "Furriers were absolutely hysterical because they have always maintained their methods are humane," she was quoted as saying in a February story printed by *The Santa Rosa Press Democrat*. "It took us a lot of blood, sweat, and tears to get behind the scenes at the LaCalle farm to show that the animals were dying in excruciating pain."

In April, *The Panama City News Herald* ran a column by Ingrid, marking World Week for Animals in Laboratories. "Pretending animals are beneath our consideration is insupportably speciesist, and pretending that abusing them will bring us a magic pill for what ails us is unrealistic," PETA's co-founder wrote. "Whether it is by using an alternative to dissection, choosing a shampoo guaranteed not to have been force-fed to rabbits, or telling your old college you will not send a check until they stop forcing pigeons and rats through mazes, everyone can do something to liberate animals from laboratories."

The Washington Post published an article in May, describing how animal activists wrote threatening letters to vivisectors, and sent, assumedly disparaging, messages to the neighbors of researchers. Ingrid defended the latter tactic while making a somewhat unconvincing nod to legality. "It's psychological warfare," she told reporter Lorraine Adams. "And it's not pleasant. If someone hides what they do, they should be able to defend it to their neighbors. It's like Nazi war criminals. It's ugly, but as long as it's not violent—because we're totally opposed to violence—we do it."

In August, *The Port Arthur News* published what seems to have originally been a story in *The New York Times*, detailing PETA's rumored plan to relocate. "The animal rights and biotechnology communities are abuzz with the news that People for the Ethical Treatment of Animals, a pro-animal group second in size to the Humane Society and much more radical, is moving its headquarters from Rockville, Md., to Seattle," the unsigned article stated, noting the rumor was also reported by Animal People and the newsletter of Northwest Animal Rights Network. "PETA will not discuss the matter."

Ingrid was the lone dissenting voice in a *Los Angeles Times* article, which ran in August, heralding the use of transgenic rodents in research. "Mice are like us in that they feel pain and fear and value their lives—that's why it's unethical to use them," Ingrid told reporter Bettijane Levine. "But they are not like us in many physiological respects. They are used [in research] because they are cheap, easy to handle and evoke very little public sympathy."

In October, *The New Braunfels Herald-Zeitung* published a letter from Ingrid, celebrating the 125th anniversary of Mohandas Gandhi's birth. "Were the Mahatma alive, we would probably find him on Larry King, urging people to stop moaning and to take positive steps to make their corner of the world a little less violent," she wrote. "Gandhi's compassion was boundless. A vegetarian who spoke out against all forms of violence, he rallied a continent to overthrow British imperialism; treated the Harijans, the lowest, 'untouchable' caste of Hindus, as brothers; and fought the maltreatment of Blacks and Asians in apartheid South Africa." She urged readers to follow Gandhi's example and abstain from flesh.

Ingrid sent a letter to the U.S. attorney general, requesting federal prisons stop serving meat, according to a November brief in *The Washington Post.* "With violent crime and prison populations soaring," Ingrid was quoted as having written, "this would create leaner budgets and more healthful, less violent inmates . . . Many violent criminals, including Jeffrey Dahmer, start as animal abusers. Feeding inmates bean burritos rather than baby back ribs would break the cycle of cruelty."

In April of 1996, *The South Holland Star* published a letter from PETA worker Carla Bennett—who, in responding to claims made by a furrier, discussed Ingrid's modest compensation. "Alex Pacheco and Ingrid Newkirk each receive $25,000 annually for their 60-hour work weeks as president and vice-president, respectively," Bennet wrote. "They receive no additional compensation for their work on PETA's board of directors." In contrast, more than five years prior, the president of the Humane Society of the United States received almost $150,000 annually, according to Norm Phelps' book, *The Longest Struggle.*

Bruce Friedrich started working for Ingrid in May. "I had been a vegan for nine years at that point, and believed in animal rights," he told this writer in a brief conversation. "I really liked the PETA, Merry Prankster, sort-of-irreverent attitude toward social justice." He was interviewed by Ingrid for approximately an hour. "We really hit it off," Bruce recounted, noting PETA's co-founder let him choose the department he wanted to work in. "So I picked campaigns."

Gillette began a moratorium on animal testing in 1996, because of PETA pressure. The chronology on the group's website described it as "colorful years-long campaign, including the presentation of shareholder resolutions at Gillette's annual meetings and support from compassionate celebrities Paul McCartney, Lily Tomlin, Hugh Grant, and Elizabeth Hurley."

In June, *The Chicago Tribune* covered a small protest that was part of this effort. "A handful of animal-rights activists gathered Tuesday outside a Bolingbrook distribution center operated by the Gillette Co. to protest the company's practice of using animals to test products," journalist Annmarie Mannion wrote. "The hourlong protest attracted about five demonstrators representing People for the Ethical Treatment of Animals, or PETA, and Illinois Animal Action Inc."

Later that month, PETA relocated—not to Seattle, but to Norfolk, Virginia. *The Garden City Telegram* ran an Associated Press brief on the move. "The lead singer of The Pretenders popped the cork off a champagne bottle Monday as she helped christen the new headquarters of People for the Ethical Treatment of Animals," the unsigned article stated. "The non-profit group is moving from Rockville, Md., a Washington suburb, to Richmond because it is centrally located on the East Coast and is less expensive than Washington, a spokesman for the group said."

In July, *The Panama City News Herald* ran a column by Ingrid, opposing zoos. "They are not educational," PETA's co-founder wrote. "They endorse domination, give us a false perspective on our place in the natural order and show animals in unnatural groups and unnatural settings." Still, she suggested such facilities could be redeemed. "Let's bring zoos into the '90s by turning them into desperately needed shelters for the shackled elephants, bicycle-riding bears and neck-chained chimpanzees who are sold to hunting ranches or put in the back room to die when they are no longer young and pretty," Ingrid argued.

PETA hired Rick Swain, a former Montgomery County police officer, to serve as executive director—according to a piece published in August by *The Cumberland Times-News*, that seems to have originally appeared in *The Prince George's Journal*. Ingrid was quoted, saying Rick's purview would include "everything and anything administrative or business" and that he would "cast half an eye to advising us on investigative strategies." Ingrid came to know Rick during the Silver Spring monkey case.

In November, *The Sedalia Democrat* ran an Associated Press article, in which Ingrid worried Disney's live-action remake of *101*

Dalmatians would lead to a spike in homeless pets, after the movie left theaters and the breed's appeal faded. "It's going to wind up to be a real-life snuff film for Dalmatians," PETA's co-founder said. "Every child in the audience is going to want one and a lot of parents will give in to them."

PETA came into conflict with another organization over the treatment of stray animals, according to an Associated Press report printed by *The Newport News Daily Press* in December. "Both groups want the cats neutered, vaccinated and fed," the unsigned report stated, noting PETA sought to take the animals. "The Meower Power League believes the cats should stay on the docks to catch rats because there aren't enough homes for them. On Wednesday, the dispute became a physical confrontation as two cat-lovers struggled for control of one trapped feline, and police were called."

Ingrid criticized the league. "She said PETA trapped two adult cats that had feline leukemia and two kittens that were anemic and had parasites," the report from the Associated Press stated. "All four were put to sleep." Ingrid spoke of the remaining animals going to warm, loving homes—but acknowledged the locations where PETA typically placed cats were full, which makes one wonder what she intended to do with the creatures.

The same year, PETA protested the National Aeronautics and Space Administration. "Following PETA's campaign, NASA [pulled] out of Bion—a joint U.S., French, and Russian experiment in which monkeys wearing straitjackets were to have electrodes implanted in their bodies and be launched into space," the chronology on PETA's website stated.

Arnauld E. Nicogossian appeared to confirm this in his book, *Space Physiology and Medicine.* "NASA's use of animal test subjects was an attractive and highly visible target for PETA's goal to eliminate biomedical research using animal test subjects," he wrote. "The publicity surrounding the Bion 11 flight resulted in several Congressional hearings and further intensified post-flight with the death of one of the primates, and ultimately led to the cancellation of U.S. funding for the remainder of the program."

8

JERRY SPRINGER AND MONICA LEWINSKY

In March of 1997, *The Sandusky Register* published a column by Ingrid, responding to news that Scottish scientists had cloned a sheep. "In all the fanciful public discussion, no one has even mentioned that it might not be ethical to treat animals like test tubes with tails," she wrote. "Apart from the fantasy of what cloning might mean for people, we need to look at what cloning experiments will mean for animals. Sheep, after all, aren't commodities to be produced like grapefruit." Ingrid concluded her piece by insisting humans shouldn't search for new ways to exploit animals.

Later that month, in a story printed by *The New York Times*, Ingrid spoke out against a university art project—in which a student killed a frog and reanimated its corpse with electrodes attached to a circuit board. "This isn't about animal rights," PETA's co-founder told journalist Bruce Weber. "It's about obeying laws that recognize gratuitous harm to living beings. You can't frivolously kill animals for art. It may be an amusement to this man Arnold, but to the frog, it's his little life."

Still in March, Ingrid was quoted in an article about feral cats, that ran in *The Washington Post*. She opposed neutering and releasing such creatures, a practice favored by some activists, as an alternative to the animals being killed in shelters. Ingrid explained that she had seen "cats torn apart by car engines, by pit bulls—the horror stories are endless. I believe once you have your hand on that stray, once you anesthetize them, why bring them back to take their chances again?"

At the end of the month, *The Cumberland Times-News* printed a letter from Ingrid, making clear not everyone was happy when animal circuses came to town. "Many people find it a sad spectacle to see once-majestic tigers reduced to being prodded out of their cages to perform silly tricks," she wrote. "Animal-free circuses like the fabulous Cirque du Soleil employ only talented human trapeze artists, jugglers, fire-eaters, and other performers. These circuses are delightfully devoid of tutu-clad bears on roller skates, whips, leg shackles, bullhooks, muzzles, electric prods, and the smell of dung."

Animal activists were suspected of releasing 10,000 mink from an Oregon fur farm, according to a June story in *USA Today*. Many of the animals were recaptured and there was a debate about whether those remaining in the wild could survive. "They were headed for a hideous death at the end of a ghastly life," Ingrid told journalist Tom Curley. "The cruelty involved in all of this is an abomination. I think it's the mink farmers who should be prosecuted."

Ingrid was opposed to the National Research Council's plan to warehouse chimpanzees formerly used in experiments. Instead— she argued in an August column, which ran in *The Logansport Pharos-Tribune*—the animals should be retired to a genuine sanctuary. "Many of these primates have decades to live," Ingrid wrote. "They need space, fresh air, sunshine and the companionship of other chimps. And our government, which has paid for their capture, breeding, and suffering in laboratories, is now responsible for putting funds into a decent retirement facility. These highly intelligent, socially complex chimpanzees, betrayed for decades by a more 'advanced' species, deserve no less."

Later that month, *The Hartford Courant* printed a story about a visit from the Oscar Mayer Wienermobile that was canceled after threats of a PETA protest. "Kids would lose their lunch if they knew what actually went into a wiener," Ingrid said. "A meat hot dog contains every imaginable 'leftover' part of an abused animal, including pig stomach, snout, intestines, spleens and, yes, even lips."

In September, *USA Today* ran a profile of a female bullfighter. Ingrid condemned the blood-sport participant in terms that revealed her belief in a certain degree of gender essentialism. "It's almost more offensive to me to see women bullfighting," PETA's co-founder told reporter Marco della Cava. "I can understand a man's biological and cultural needs. But for women to have the need to control an animal to the extent of slaughtering it well, I think they should all be in psychoanalysis."

According to an October article in *The New York Times*, Ingrid was surprised by what she saw as the media's gullibility—in accepting furriers' narrative, that their product was making a resurgence. "Fur is not back," she told journalist Jennifer Steinhauer. "We are pretty flabbergasted that the fashion press has picked up on the fur industry's constant barrage."

Later that month, *The Baltimore Sun* ran a story about a shopping mall that was essentially installing a zoo inside its premises. Ingrid made clear that she was not impressed by the exploitative spectacle. "It's all rather pathetic," she said to reporter Mary Corey. "Animals aren't living toys. They're not here for our amusement. The way you respect wildlife is to leave it alone—afford it its natural life."

Ingrid spoke about the Animal Liberation Front in blunt terms, in a December article printed in *The New York Daily News*. "I will be the last person to condemn ALF," PETA's co-founder said, adding no one had been physically injured by the group's clandestine attacks. "Would I rather the research lab that tests animals is reduced to a bunch of cinders? Yes." Still, Ingrid didn't seem pleased with the ALF's direction. "In the early '90s, it was a very different group, well-organized, and generated a lot of sympathy," she said. "Now they're just angry, and act without planning."

That same month, *The Winchester Star* published an Associated Press piece, reporting Huntingdon Life Sciences settled a lawsuit against PETA. "PETA must return or destroy all the information an undercover PETA worker took from the lab," the unsigned article stated. "It may not interfere with the lab's business relationships with its clients, nor suggest to anyone that they should not hire the lab. PETA also is barred from any undercover information-gathering against the lab for five years."

However, the animal group didn't have to pay any damages to the vivisection company or admit wrongdoing. "We didn't exactly give away the farm, and we did not pay them a penny," Ingrid was quoted as saying, in the same Associated Press piece. "We won a great deal for the animals in that Colgate canceled its contract with Huntingdon, and Procter & Gamble launched an independent investigation that led to its denouncement of Huntingdon's animal-handling practices."

When a camel was killed by a car after escaping from a Nativity pageant, Ingrid noted other animals were harmed at similar events. "The camel had no business being there," Ingrid said in a late December article in *The Washington Post*. "We get lambs attacked by dogs. We've had Nativity animals stabbed and beaten up by juveniles. We had a case where a sheep became overheated when the sun came out."

In January of 1998, an Associated Press brief was printed in *The Titusville Herald*, reporting PETA was giving away fur coats to the homeless. "We've buried them, burned them, spray-painted them and now we're giving them away," Ingrid said. Another PETA spokesperson was quoted in the piece, arguing the poor was the only segment of the population that still had an excuse to wear fur. "We can't bring the animals back, but we can bring a little warmth to people in desperate need," activist Debbie Chissell said.

Ingrid discussed hunting with hounds, in a March article published by *The Washington Post*, about a proposed ban on the practice in England. PETA's London office had pushed for the measure. "Foxhunting is a scurrilous little throwback," Ingrid told reporter Maria Glod. "Why not just take the family cat and terrorize it until it goes to ground? It's just not a decent thing to do." She added PETA didn't agitate against foxhunting in the United States, because it wasn't very common here.

Following a PETA complaint, HLS was charged by the U.S. Department of Agriculture with violating the Animal Welfare Act, according to an Associated Press piece that ran in *The Harrisonburg Daily News-Record* in April. Ingrid cheered this development. "It couldn't have happened to a more well-deserving group of money-grubbing animal abusers," she said. Later that month, *The New York Times* stated HLS settled with the Department of Agriculture—paying a $50,000 fine while admitting no wrongdoing. Ingrid chalked this up as a win. "Any improvement is a victory for us if we've been able to help to achieve it," she said.

Ingrid criticized Disney's recently-opened Animal Kingdom, in a May column for *The Fort Lauderdale Sun-Sentinel*. "Thirteen 're-portable' animals, members of the few species Disney is required by federal regulation to keep track of, had perished even before the paint had dried on the ticket windows," she wrote. "Of these, two were run over by safari buses, two died painfully from drinking anti-freeze and two were poisoned by eating dangerous plants. Disney dismissed the deaths as 'to be expected' when you have 1,000 individuals in your care, an excuse I suspect wouldn't fly with parents if the company ever opened a day-care center."

Later that month, PETA handed over the domain RinglingBrothers. com to the famous circus, after Ringling threatened to sue the animal group for copyright infringement. "On the Web site, PETA had posted a page stating it was not affiliated with the circus," journalist Matt Richtel wrote in *The New York Times* that month. "It then detailed instances in which the Government has found Ringling out of compliance with animal care regulations." Unsurprisingly, Ingrid was unapologetic. It appears her organization may have gotten the domain-squatting idea from someone who registered PETA. org to launch a 'People Eating Tasty Animals' parody site.

Ingrid reiterated her commitment to publicity stunts in an Associated Press article published by *The New Bern Sun Journal* in August. "Our job is to make sure we get attention to our issues," she said, noting this could be difficult in a country focused on Jerry Springer and Monica Lewinsky. "In the good old days, the news wasn't just bombarded to you from all corners of the earth, with all sorts of titillation. Today, you have to fight very hard to take a piece of that action."

Ingrid continued in The Associated Press piece, arguing there weren't significant negative effects from PETA's headline-grabbing approach. "No one's going to go out and buy an extra steak because we are dumping manure in front of the Beef Trade Association meeting," she said. "For five minutes, people will make fun of us, and then for ten minutes, we'll get to talk about vegetarianism."

The mainstream media forced PETA into a no-win situation, insisted Jane Velez-Mitchell. "We will not cover the serious issues that you raise about vivisection, about animal agriculture, about fur or even SeaWorld," the television journalist told this writer. "But if you do something provocative—like have some women in a tub, covered in paint to look like orcas—we'll cover it. Then we'll criticize you for doing outlandish things."

In August, *The Alamogordo Daily News* ran an Associated Press report, detailing the Air Force's plan to give a group of research chimpanzees to an animal-testing facility. Ingrid said she'd prefer the primates be put to death than suffer further experimentation. "It's sort of a battlefield decision," she said. "Would you rather stand by and see them tortured or would you like to end it quickly and painlessly?" For reasons not entirely clear, she didn't push for all the chimpanzees to go to a sanctuary—as she had with the Silver Spring monkeys.

Ingrid requested General Mills remove a champion bass fisherman's image from Wheaties boxes, according to what appears to have been an Associated Press brief, printed in *The Fairbanks Daily News-Miner*. "Anglers have no place next to real sportsmen like Michael Jordan and Tiger Woods, who better represent the breakfast of champions," she said. "Tricking small animals into impaling themselves on hooks and ripping them from their homes—from the comfort of an expensive boat—requires no athletic skill whatsoever."

That year, PETA successfully campaigned for the passage of Taiwan's first anti-cruelty law, according to the chronology on the organization's website. An article published in September by CBSNews.com provided further information about the fight. "PETA says thousands of strays in Taiwan are being electrocuted, starved, poisoned, and buried alive in dog pounds because no law prohibits cruelty to animals," CBSNews.com staff reported. "Protesters say they plan to gather outside the Taipei Economic and Cultural Office on Second Avenue [in New York City] to release never-before-seen video footage shot last month showing dogs left to die of starvation, tied by metal nooses inside makeshift pens."

In October, *The Wall Street Journal* ran a story about a PETA advertisement targeting Procter & Gamble for using animals in product testing. With text reading 'some big bright packages contain dirty little secrets,' the promotion featured a drag queen holding a parody box of Tide laundry detergent. Ingrid explained the thinking behind this act of culture jamming, which some progressives might regard as offensive. "We have to reach the consumer," she said.

"We want to incorporate our message into their jingles. Whenever anyone hears or sees Tide, we want them to think of our ads."

Later that month, *The Wisconsin State Journal* published a brief about Ingrid petitioning the governor to change the state beverage from cow milk. "Milk is white liquid tobacco, and mucus is king in Wisconsin," she said. "Governor Thompson may not care about dairy cows, who have been turned into milk machines, but we hoped he would consider their male babies, cruelly raised for veal. Consumers should remember: There is a hunk of veal in every glass of milk."

In November, *The London Independent* printed an article about Ingrid, who was visiting England. "She is currently protesting at the South African embassy in London about the export to the US and Europe of baby elephants," reporter Mary Braid wrote. "She likens their enforced separation—'while they weep'—from their mothers to the barbarities of the slave trade." Braid continued, discussing PETA's reputation in the United Kingdom. "The organization has failed to make a comparable impact in this country," Braid wrote. "While British groups claim to admire Newkirk's commitment and PETA's creative campaigns, privately they complain that the group is 'hit and run,' raising issues but seldom building on them."

E magazine ran a piece about Henry Spira, who had recently died from esophageal cancer, in its November/December issue. "He was a wonderful activist, but we would butt heads periodically," Ingrid was quoted as saying. "We felt sometimes he was too soft. We refuse to negotiate with McDonald's, for instance. Henry would sit in their corporate boardroom, while we had a picket line outside." This was ironic, given PETA's upcoming campaign to secure basic welfare improvements from the fast-food company.

Around 1998, Scotlund Haisley, who would go on to launch Animal Rescue Corp, accompanied Ingrid and her assistant on another trip abroad. "They were working on some other projects in India—some projects that had to do with exposing the leather trade," he recalled in an interview with this author. "There was a lot of traveling that they had to do. So I was doing these shelter assessments in the communities that they traveled to."

Scotlund believed the trip laid the groundwork for the formation of PETA India. "This was the first time, to my knowledge, that

Ingrid started putting time, energy and resources into India," he told this author. "We started meeting a lot of people." One of these was Maneka Gandhi, a member of the Nehru-Gandhi family, who founded People for Animals. "She was fantastic," Scotlund recalled. "I learned a lot from her."

9

THE BRAINS AND BALLS
OF THE OUTFIT

In January of 1999, Ingrid was quoted in *The New York Times*, saying money spent reducing the number of homeless animals put to death could be used more efficiently. "The people who are coming to fund the no-kill shelters obviously have high hopes and big hearts—and deep pockets," she told reporter Evelyn Nieves. "But every day, I pray that some of that money will go to the unpopular roots of the problem."

Ingrid continued, in the same *New York Times* piece, arguing the no-kill movement's goals were ultimately unobtainable. "We cannot condemn the shelters that do euthanize when there are animals who would be suffering on the streets if shelters couldn't bring them in because they had no room," she said. "I don't think there will ever be world peace, and I don't think we'll ever have a no-kill nation."

Jim Mason told this writer that Ingrid's readiness to put healthy animals to death was incongruent with an animal-rights message. "If animal lives matter as much as we claim, then we ought to go to more trouble," he said. "So, you don't just put them to sleep. You find homes. You promote spaying and neutering. You do everything you can to stop this mindless killing."

Later in January, PETA issued a media statement, announcing a lawsuit against police and school officials, who prevented the organization from protesting McDonalds' sponsorship of Eisenhower Junior High School. "It is a crime that a public school is promoting a corporation that is cruel to animals and exploits children," Ingrid said. "If they fly the McDonald's flag, it needs to be at half-mast to mark the death of nutrition education."

In Denmark, PETA activists were arrested preemptively, according to a February press release on the website of the group's United Kingdom affiliate. "Jailed for 24 hours, threatened with six days of imprisonment and deportation, denied access to legal advice and embassy representation, the women were only released after the fur auction ended," the release stated. This surprised Ingrid, who wasn't among those taken into custody. "Our protests have taken us to the streets in Paris, New York, and Taiwan—we've even marched naked through Red Square and Hong Kong—but we have never experienced such bizarre arrest and imprisonment," she said.

In March, *The Cincinnati Enquirer* reported John Pepper—the retired CEO of Procter & Gamble—had personally reached out to Ingrid, to stop a campaign against him. "Early last month, two PETA members, protesting Cincinnati-based P&G's limited use of animals to test some products, smashed tofu cream pies in Mr. Pepper's face during a speech he was giving at Northwestern University," journalist Randy Tucker wrote. "Mr. Pepper, who remains chairman of the consumer-products company, was the target of a similar attack in February 1998, when a PETA protester hit him in the face with a pie as he received an award from Ohio's governor in Columbus."

The same article in *The Cincinnati Enquirer* quoted a response Ingrid sent to Pepper, who had apparently promised to consider a moratorium on animal testing. "I will ask our grass-roots campaigners to leave you in peace," PETA's co-founder wrote. "Please do what you need to do to make sure that I have done the right thing by bringing you the peace of mind you requested."

Later that month, *The New York Post* ran a short piece on the backlash to an epithet used by some animal activists. "The Stonewall Republicans, a gay rights group for GOPers, has written to PETA asking them to stop using the term 'fur hag,' for such fur-wearing women as Anna Wintour," the unsigned piece stated. "The Stonewallers feel it's too reminiscent of the term 'fag hag' and draws the parallel that women who are friends with gay men are as villainous as those who wear fur." Ingrid didn't seem to be moved by the request. "I have been called a lot of things in my time, but one I am proud of is 'fag hag,'" she said.

In April, *USA Today* caught up with Ingrid about a party celebrating the release of her book, *You Can Save the Animals.* The event, scheduled to take place at actor Woody Harrelson's restaurant, had a celebrity guest list that included Pamela Anderson Lee, Bill Maher, Richard Pryor, and Sporty Spice. "If I get 600 people who each do one kind thing because of this, then I'm really happy," PETA's cofounder told journalist Jeannie Williams. "We'll have natural juices, and special finger foods, not fingers, veggie stuff. Woody has always been a vegan. He eats no animal products."

Ingrid suggested zoonoses were akin to karmic retribution, in a column printed by *The Jacksonville Journal-Courier* in June. "Mad cow disease may come as a nasty surprise to us privileged beings, but to the cow, it is just one more man-made misery," she wrote, following an advisory from the U.S. Food and Drug Administration about the zoonosis. "If what goes around comes around, the revenge of the cows may be far more devastating than the Ebola virus or swine flu."

Procter & Gamble agreed to restrict its animal experimentation to some degree, according to a July article in *The Cincinnati Enquirer.* "We will refocus our campaign against Procter & Gamble because they will no longer conduct tests on existing products," Ingrid said. "But if P&G puts a new product on the market or comes up with a brand-spanking new ingredient, they will not promise to spare animals' lives. So we will warn consumers to stay away from any new P&G products."

In a column published later that month by *The Jacksonville Journal-Courier*, Ingrid discussed a recent legal first—the indictment of factory-farm workers on felony-cruelty charges. This was made possible by an undercover PETA video, which revealed the men beating lame pigs. "They screamed obscenities at them with each blow of the hammer, metal gate post, boot or heavy rod," Ingrid wrote. "In one scene, they take out one of those little window scraper blades and start to skin a sow while she's still alive." She didn't believe this was out of the ordinary. "My bet is you'd see similar scenes in most, if not every, pig farm in the country," she said. "The problem is that you can't get into these pig fortresses except on a white glove tour."

In August, PETA sent out a press release, announcing a $50,000 grant to the Institute for In Vitro Science. "IIVS, a laboratory and

testing facility devoted to modernizing test methods, is the first recipient of a $250,000 'End of the Century' grant that PETA will
disburse," the release stated. "The grants are intended to speed up
the process by which highly predictive cell tests are accepted by
government regulatory agencies such as the EPA and FDA."

Ingrid hoped this would inspire others to finance such efforts.
"We are putting our money where our mouth is to haul science out
of the Dark Ages and leave animal tests in the dust," she said in
the same release. "The work of IIVS and other pioneers deserves
our support and the support of these industries and agencies. This
is a challenge to all users of animals in crude tests to get out their
checkbooks."

The Smithsonian canceled a foie-gras tasting following an activist
protest, according to a *Chicago Daily Herald* brief which ran later
that month. Ingrid called the decision long overdue. "Foie gras production is an old and cruel process," she said. "It has no place in
an institution like the Smithsonian, except in the history part of the
museum." A spokesman for the Smithsonian hinted the backlash
to the event had included threats of violence.

Still in August, *The Baltimore Sun* printed a column by Ingrid,
slamming presidential candidate Al Gore for supporting vivisection.
"Why is the vice president pushing for slaughter when more ac-
curate, humane methods are available?" PETA's co-founder wrote.
"We will continue to send a 6-foot 'rabbit' to follow Mr. Gore wher-
ever he goes. At least until enough humanitarians, environmental-
ists and sensible taxpayers demand—and get—an immediate end
to this ill-conceived plan to poison millions of animals."

That fall, Peter Singer began facing protests due to his belief parents
should be able to put severely-handicapped newborns to death.
"Some people have attacked me for those things, and said I was not
a good spokesperson for the animal movement because of my views
about euthanasia," the philosopher told this writer. "Ingrid's been a
great supporter on that—and a rational voice in that debate—where
some other people have been a little more hysterical."

Ingrid backed an effort by New York City Mayor Rudy Giuliani to
defund a Brooklyn Museum of Art exhibit. "Damien Hirst, one of

the featured artists, wants us to buy into his tidy disclaimer that the animal bodies used in his pieces for the exhibition were 'already dead,' PETA's co-founder wrote in a letter *Newsday* published in October. "While it is true that Hirst didn't wield the cleaver, he might as well have. The cow and her calf, and the sheep, pigs and other animals he pickled and cut through with a chainsaw didn't die in their sleep."

Later that month, *The Atlanta Journal-Constitution* ran a message from Ingrid, saying she wouldn't be surprised if animal activists were responsible for threatening letters—lined with razor blades—which were mailed to vivisectionists. "After more than 100 years of writing polite letters and demonstrating peacefully, and despite all we have learned about our fellow primates, monkeys used in experiments are still denied all recognition of their intelligence, family structure, and basic interests," she wrote. "Perhaps the mere idea of receiving a nasty missive will allow animal researchers to empathize with their victims for the first time in their lousy careers."

Ingrid acknowledged her past role as informal spokeswoman for the Animal Liberation Front, in a December article published by *The Atlanta Journal-Constitution.* "The ALF used to send us tapes, photos of animals they had rescued, reports on research protocol, you name it," she said. "We always turned them over to the government, the press, Congress, the public, so people could judge for themselves. They were sent to us anonymously, because they know we'd put them out. We don't know who these people were, and they're smart, staying anonymous. There are serious consequences if they're caught."

In the same article from *The Atlanta-Journal Constitution,* Ingrid expressed clear admiration for the ALF. "I wish all of us had the nerve to get up and go into labs and fur farms and get the animals out," she said. "But we don't. Hopefully, enough of us will do something legal, which is all PETA ever espouses, except for civil disobedience, upon which this country was founded." Ingrid insisted her organization didn't engage in some other forms of aggressive activism. "We have done street theater in which we used paint-splattered donated furs on our own models," she said. "Of course, paint has been smeared on fur wearers (by others), but we do not do it or advocate it."

Still in December, PETA distributed a press release on the day *Vogue* editor Anna Wintour attended her father's funeral. "[She] has rejected all appeals to consider how cruel it is to drown, electrocute, and bludgeon animals for their skins," Ingrid said. "Our hope is that on this one day she may be capable of empathy and turn her personal distress into a positive experience for the countless animals who suffer only because of her insensitivity."

That same month, *The South China Morning Post* ran a story in which Ingrid slammed the city of Little Rock, Arkansas, for putting money towards the development of Bill Clinton's presidential library. PETA's co-founder believed the funds could be better spent improving animal welfare at the local zoo. "I would say that the Little Rock Zoo is the worst in the entire country," she told reporter Liz Hodgson. "Those poor animals are starving and abused. The idea that money is going to be taken away from them to fund Clinton's library is an abomination."

Also in 1999, Pacheco left PETA. According to Hershaft, Pacheco said he was forced out. "He told me the way he found out that he was no longer running PETA is that PETA had a gala in Los Angeles," Hershaft claimed, in an interview with this writer. "He was working his way to the stage to make his speech and the guard wouldn't let him." Hershaft believed this was Ingrid's doing. "Alex had some personal issues with alcohol," he said. "So that could have been a reason."

Bruce didn't remember Pacheco being actively engaged with the organization. "To the degree that he was involved, it was pretty figurehead," Bruce said in a conversation this writer. "He would be occasionally around the office—an incredibly nice, friendly, funny dude, but not involved in the day-to-day at all." Still, Bruce didn't know the circumstances of Pacheco's departure.

Pacheco insisted leaving was his choice. "After twenty years I left for several reasons, the majority of which revolved around differences of opinion on how best to carry out animal protection work," he told this author in a limited interview. "For example, I was very much in support of spending more time and resources on lobbying members of Congress for animal protection, and she felt otherwise, at least at that time." Pacheco added he and Ingrid disagreed about the value of negative press attention.

Speaking with this writer, Dan Mathews remembered Pachecho's exit in much the same way. "He was moving in the direction of more lobbying," Dan said. "We were moving in the direction of more agitation. It became very clear that the larger, more conservative groups were better at lobbying. PETA is a bit of a hot potato."

While Karen Davis didn't know the details surrounding Pacheco's departure, she suggested it was inevitable Ingrid would win any sort of power struggle with him. "There's no question that Ingrid was the stronger personality, more dedicated personality," Karen said in an interview with this writer. "If it was going to be between Alex and Ingrid, Ingrid was going to come out on top—which is good . . . I think Alex has subsequently shown that he was not on the level of Ingrid."

Discussing his observations of the pair during PETA's early years, Jim made a similar point. "My sense of Alex was he just didn't measure up," he recalled. "They just weren't really that equal in terms of competence, ambition, [and] work ethic. Alex, relatively speaking, seemed to be more of a slacker. Ingrid was the brains and balls of the outfit."

10

A LEAN, MEAN FIGHTING MACHINE

In 2000, according to the chronology on PETA's website, the group convinced many retailers to boycott leather from China and India, after a PETA investigation found conditions in those countries to be particularly egregious. *The New York Post* covered the campaign in a March piece. "It was back on the chain gang for singer Chrissie Hynde of The Pretenders yesterday—she was put behind bars after leading animal activists in invading a Midtown Gap store to rip apart leather jackets," reporter Angela C. Allen wrote, referencing one of the singer's hit songs. "Hynde, PETA President Ingrid Newkirk, and two male protesters were charged with criminal mischief."

That year, PETA donated $5,000 to the Josh Harper Support Committee, according to Don Liddick's book *Eco-terrorism.* "I was subpoenaed to a grand jury in Portland, Oregon, that was investigating actions that had been undertaken by the Animal Liberation Front and Earth Liberation Front," Josh recalled in an interview with this author. "I sent an open letter to the prosecutor, basically saying that I was not going to help him."

The Seattle-based activist was charged with criminal contempt of a grand jury. "I put out a call at that time for assistance paying for my legal fees," Josh told this writer, noting the committee representing him approached Ingrid. "Many, many months went by and we didn't hear anything." Faced with mounting legal bills, he emailed Ingrid directly. "It was at a point where I was about to lose my attorney," Josh said. "Things had gotten desperate enough that I needed some sort of support from an institution, rather than just individual donors."

PETA subsequently sent a check. "I don't want to sound like I was ungrateful for her help," Josh said in an interview with this author. "But there was a part of me that felt like it could have come a little bit sooner." For him, the delayed donation was representative of something more. "There was a frustration on my part at that time with a lot of the national organizations—and with PETA in particular," Josh said. "I had watched over a number of years as their support for direct-action activities was in decline. [Ingrid] seemed to be distancing herself from a radical portion of the movement that she had once been a part of herself."

Around 2000, Karen Davis was dealing with rodents at the United Poultry Concerns sanctuary. "Rats were just sauntering around the yard in broad daylight," she told this writer. "They were eating up half of all the food I was buying for the chickens. They were gnawing at everything, and they were multiplying because they had no predators. They had an endless food supply of grains and seeds." Karen didn't know what to do. "I was constantly trying to get help from people," she said. "I was being tortured not only by the rats themselves but also by the moral feeling against poisoning them."

Karen learned about another sanctuary, which experienced a rodent problem. "The health department moved in, and told them that they would confiscate all their animals—they had more than just birds—and close down the sanctuary if they didn't get rid of the rats immediately," she said in an interview with this author. "We were headed in that direction." Ultimately, Karen decided to kill the rodents. "My first obligation was to our birds and to our organization," she said. "Sometimes you have to make an unhappy decision."

After finding out about this and other issues, Ingrid sent Karen an email. "She said, [a UPC worker] told her that the structure wasn't safe, that we were running what amounted to a factory farm in our kitchen by not euthanizing birds who were sick, and then we exterminated the rats," Karen recalled to this writer. "She said, the way to handle the rats is you should enclose your entire sanctuary in rat wire and have the ground covered in cement, like a prison camp." Ingrid also insisted Karen should move into a trailer, which PETA would provide. "She said, if you don't comply with what I'm telling you, I'm going to bring UPC down," Karen stated.

UPC's founder wrote back, mentioning she came from a family of lawyers and would take legal action if Ingrid attacked the organization. "I said to her, Ingrid, you've never even been to our property," Karen recalled. "I said, we have nothing to hide here; you can come right on over." Speaking with this author, UPC's founder noted she contacted Gary Baverstock, who had previously managed PETA's Aspin Hill sanctuary. "He said, when we had the sanctuary in Aspin Hill, we developed a rat problem too," Karen stated. "He said, under Ingrid's own authority, we exterminated the rats." (Attempts to interview Gary for this book were unsuccessful.)

While Gene Baur, the co-founder of Farm Sanctuary, didn't know the details of Ingrid's conflict with Karen, he said PETA tried to address animal-welfare issues at various sanctuaries. "I honestly wish that their time was spent more on dealing with animal abusers in an exploitation industry," he told this writer. "Animal sanctuaries, in some cases, are actually trying to do good—but they just get over their head. There are also times when you have animal exploiters who try to position themselves as sanctuaries. In those cases, it makes a lot of sense to go in and bust them." Gene added that hoarding was a legitimate concern as well.

In January of 2000, *The Washington Post* ran a short piece about a recent episode of *The Late Show with David Letterman*, in which the first lady and Senate-hopeful Hillary Clinton told the host she'd had her cat declawed. Ingrid condemned the decision. "Declawing is like taking a hatchet to a hangnail," PETA's co-founder said. "The surgery involves ten separate, painful amputations, severing not just the nails, but the whole joint. It is too late for Socks, but we beg you to use your position to speak out against declawing."

According to a March brief in *The New York Post*, Ingrid defended a PETA advertisement "that showed a woman's unshaven panty line with the tagline, 'Fur Trim, Unattractive.'" The image had drawn criticism from the president of the New York chapter of the National Organization for Women. "Since we left the '60s style of unshaven leg hair and bushes behind, most people like the groomed look better," Ingrid wrote. "It's not sexist, it's just a fact. Please stop this knee-jerk, reactionary rubbish. There are a lot of women out there—including longtime feminists like me—who don't appreciate being spoken to in this repressive way."

Ingrid advocated killing and banning pit bulls in a May column published *The Cedar Rapids Gazette*. "We have a file drawer chock-full of accounts of attacks in which these ill-treated dogs have torn the faces and fingers off infants and even police officers trying to serve warrants," she said, adding those who opposed putting pit bulls to death were naive. "We can only stop killing pits if we stop creating new ones. Legislators, please take note."

In July, PETA sent out a press release, expressing approval for *The Perfect Storm*, a film which used only rubber and animatronic fish during production. "*The Perfect Storm* sets a new standard in a town not known for its ethics," Ingrid said. "If there were an Oscar for compassion, [director] Wolfgang Petersen would be a shoo-in."

Later that month, *The Washington Post* reported that PETA had put to death 1,325 companion animals the previous year—out of 2,103 dogs and cats the group accepted. PETA found homes for 386 animals, while reclamations and transfers made up much of the remaining difference. Ingrid defended the organization's kill rate. "It is a totally rotten business, but sometimes the only kind option for some animals is to put them to sleep forever," she said. "I don't think a dog living in a cage walking in circles for the rest of its life in a dog prison is a swell thing."

Speaking with this writer, Ronnie Lee seemed sympathetic to Ingrid's predicament. "If you've got so many spaces for animals to go into in shelters, and far more animals than that looking for places in shelters, then what's going to happen is some of those animals are going to be put down," he said. "If the no-kill shelters don't do it, it's going to happen elsewhere." Ronnie saw this as a problem which shelters had been unfairly tasked with solving. "It's been imposed on them by public behavior," he said. "People irresponsibly breed these animals."

Still, Ronnie said PETA shouldn't have engaged in sheltering. "I tend to think it was a mistake," he told this writer. "I don't really think campaigning organizations should be involved in rescue." Ronnie believed the controversy surrounding PETA's sheltering efforts distracted from the organization's activism. "It has harmed their campaigning," he said. "It's meant that people who are opposed to them putting animals down would no longer support them or would no longer support their campaigns."

In August, *The Washington Post* printed an article about animal-welfare improvements mandated by McDonald's. "McDonald's

Corp. sent letters to the farmers who supply the company with 1.5 billion eggs yearly outlining strict new regulations for raising hens," journalist Marc Kaufman wrote. "The guidelines require 50 percent more space for each caged hen, ban the controversial practice of withholding food and water to increase egg production, and require a gradual phasing out of the 'debeaking' that is common in the poultry industry." PETA took credit for pushing the change in the chronology posted to the organization's website.

Paul Shapiro argued this was an important development. "I think some of the key advancements that PETA made on farm animals, back around the turn of the century, really helped set the stage for other advancements for farm animals," he told this writer. "Those campaigns got very modest advancements for chickens. They were increased cage sizes, no starvation and so on. But they were the first time any major food retailers had ever demanded anything from their suppliers on the treatment of chickens."

According to Bruce, even after successful campaigns, Ingrid saw her work as inadequate. "Everything for Ingrid is a mix of—this is a great victory—and—holy shit, there are still billions of animals suffering beyond any of our worst nightmares," he said in an interview with this author. "She runs a Merry Prankster organization. But she also, I think, feels the suffering of animals at an extraordinarily-deep level. So I think all celebrations and pleasure are significantly tempered by just the fact of overwhelming animal suffering, every moment of every day, everywhere."

Around 2000, Noel Ward died of prostate cancer, Bruce was quoted as saying in a CNN transcript of a late August segment. In *Making Kind Choices*, Ingrid recalled how her dad spent his final years. "If you browse among the shelves at the public library in the little Oregon town where my father died, you will see a plaque in remembrance of Noel Ward," she wrote. "When he passed away, my mother made a modest donation to the library where my father had spent so many contented hours, finding books about the war, about the sea, about electronics, about computers. He knew all the staff and liked them."

According to Bruce, in the aforementioned CNN transcript, Noel's death inspired Ingrid to create an aggressive spoof of the famous 'Got Milk?' advertisement campaign. PETA's billboards included the text "Got Prostate Cancer?" over an image of New York Mayor Rudy Giuliani, who suffered from the disease. This was apparently in reference to a Harvard study, which suggested dairy consumption might increase the risk of prostate cancer. In a September article, published in *The Wisconsin State Journal*, The Associated Press said PETA pulled the advertisements and apologized to the mayor.

That same month, *The Chicago Tribune* reported the National Highway Traffic Safety Administration had mistakenly included animal deaths among the human fatalities linked to faulty Firestone tires. Ingrid was displeased when the government corrected the error. "If these animals were in the car, they were obviously family members, not groceries," PETA's co-founder said. "Death is death, and I think they should keep them in."

Demonstrating just how toxic its reputation had become, PETA issued a press release in November, announcing talk-show host Oprah Winfrey's charity, Angel Network, had rejected a donation of $100,000 worth of non-leather shoes—out of fear of being associated with the animal group. "We love Oprah. I've been on her show, and she's a kind person," Ingrid said. "It was a chance to help animals and people at the same time." PETA ultimately gave the shoes to the Salvation Army.

In December, *The Newport News Daily Press* ran what appears to have been a story originally printed in *The Virginian-Pilot*, featuring several former PETA employees who described the organization's work environment as hostile. Ingrid pushed back on these accounts. "We have disgruntled employees who've left here," she said, adding workers were fired for good cause. "There is a little club of disgruntled employees." Still, Ingrid acknowledged she could be tough. "I believe we should be—and I say this at staff meetings—a lean, mean fighting machine," PETA's co-founder said. "This is not a rest home for people who just have warm feelings about animals."

Also in 2000, PETA India was established. According to documents uploaded to the blog of M.S. Ezhil—chief governance officer of Kiran Global Chem—Mary Ward, Ingrid's mother, was on the board of the new organization. It should be noted that Ezhil opposed PETA's efforts to ban the abusive practice jallikattu. (Attempts to speak with him about the documents were unsuccessful.)

Jon Bockman didn't think Mary's role on the board of PETA India was necessarily problematic. "It depends on the specific situation," the executive director of Animal Charity Evaluators told this writer. Writing on his blog, Ezhil seemed unaware of the relationship between Ingrid and Mary. However, he did point out Mary's signature on PETA India documents varied greatly over the years, suggesting someone was signing for her.

In January 2001, *The New York Post* reported that Ingrid wrote to Donald Trump, condemning a golfer who attacked a swan at one of the future president's courses. "The individual responsible should be prosecuted to the fullest extent of the law," PETA's co-founder said in the letter. "Our office has been fielding calls from people outraged by this senseless crime." Trump banned the golfer from all his properties, according to a brief printed in *The Philadelphia Daily News* the next day.

Later that month, Ingrid was quoted in *The Washington Post*, predicting the recent vote of Britain's House of Commons to ban fox-hunting would lead to increased opposition to blood-sport enthusiasts in the United States. "Eventually they will be seriously protested," she said. "Any cruelty we're opposed to. You'd have to have a heart like a steel trap to pursue foxes."

On the same day, PETA issued a press release, pushing for regulation of aquafarming. "Fish raised in captivity are confined to crowded, unnatural conditions that cause stress and lead to outbreaks of disease," the release stated. "To control parasites, skin and gill infections, and other diseases, aquaculturists routinely pump fish full of antibiotics and chemicals—which often end up in local waterways." Ingrid wanted this to change. "While fish cannot express their suffering in ways people readily recognize, you don't have to be a marine biologist to realize that they do indeed feel pain," she said. "The government's inaction regarding aquafarming has led to fouled waterways and a new dimension in fish misery."

In February, Ingrid's organization distributed a media statement, blasting the reality-show *Survivor*, in which participants killed nonhumans. "Last year, CBS made contestants torture and eat rats, rays, and chickens," PETA's co-founder said. "Now, they've decapitated a rooster and stabbed a pig to death. The ratings wars have created a bloody battlefield: by their choice of contestants, the stakes dangled in front of them, and the cruelty inspired or even required, someone at CBS needs to be prosecuted."

Somewhat dispiritingly, Ingrid couldn't imagine a time when PETA was unnecessary, according to a March profile in *The Australian*. "That day will never dawn," she was quoted as saying. "It's like the peace movement or working against child abuse . . . you know in your heart it will never happen." Still, PETA's co-founder joked about the circumstances that would motivate her to give up the animals' struggle. "If Burger King promised to become a vegetarian restaurant if I retired, I'd retire," she said. "I'd go to the beach and order piña coladas."

The Medicine Hat News printed an article in April from The Canadian Press, reporting Ingrid claimed there were upsides to the spread of foot-and-mouth disease. "Newkirk said an outbreak in Britain has prompted measures for which her organization had pushed for decades, including bans on livestock markets, factory farming and prolonged and frequent transport of animals," the unsigned piece stated. This led Canadian authorities to fear the threat of bioterrorism.

In June, *The New York Times* ran a story about reaction to an essay by Peter Singer, in which the philosopher argued bestiality could be ethical. While some animal advocates pointed out animals couldn't meaningfully consent to sex with humans, Ingrid seemed to entertain Peter's view. "If a girl gets sexual pleasure from riding a horse, does the horse suffer?" PETA's co-founder said. "If not, who cares? If you French kiss your dog and he or she thinks it's great, is it wrong?"

Later that month, *The Whitehorse Star* published a letter from Ingrid, addressing reports right-wing terrorist Timothy McVeigh abstained from flesh in the days leading up to his execution. PETA's co-founder painted this as a momentous choice. "Odd as it seems, Timothy McVeigh might end up being a good 'poster child' for vegetarianism," Ingrid wrote. "If a man like him can reflect, change, then openly speak of wanting to bring peace, as McVeigh did, it brings great hope to those of us who work to stop violence in every part of our society, including in the slaughterhouse. Surely 'ordinary' people can do as much, and reject killing?"

Still in June, *The Calgary Herald* printed a piece about designer pets. "An American company plans to produce kittens with 'deleted' allergy genes," journalist Chris Ayres wrote. "They will be sold for about $1,100 to people who normally suffer runny eyes, sneezing and breathing difficulties in feline company." Unsurprisingly, Ingrid seemed to oppose this. "We tinker with animals and then we learn what we mucked up and can't fix it," she said. "There are many things you can do if you are allergic to cats. You can have good ventilation, use a wet vacuum cleaner, have someone else brush them, and feed them a good diet."

That year, PETA secured commitments to animal-welfare reform from Burger King and Wendy's, according to PETA's chronology. A July article posted to the United Press International website covered some of the efforts which led to the change. "The day before the July 4 holiday, animal rights activists Tuesday staged a declaration of independence for commercially bred livestock, resulting in five arrests at a Wendy's restaurant," journalist Mike Martin wrote. "The protest over the treatment of animals used for food production was sponsored by People for the Ethical Treatment of Animals, or PETA, and drew more than 150 demonstrators, many from the Animal Rights 2001 conference at the Hilton Hotel in nearby McLean."

In August, *The Medicine Hat News* ran a letter from Ingrid, praising a decision by the Canadian Veterinary Medical Association, which called for legislation to end the practice of declawing cats. "The procedure involves removing not just the claws or nails, but bone and muscle tissue, the first phalange on every claw," she wrote. "Claws being like fingers to cats, imagine having the last joint of your own fingers removed and you get the idea."

PETA sent out a press release in early September, denouncing research financed by the March of Dimes. "Philanthropists will be shocked that money they give to help babies may be used to harm monkeys instead," Ingrid said. "We want them to insist that the March of Dimes fund prenatal care and a birth-defect prevention registry, not torture infant animals."

Following the September 11 terrorist attacks, Ingrid promised to tone down PETA's tactics, according to an Associated Press brief published that month by *The Bluefield Daily Telegraph*. It's unclear from the piece if this was supposed to be a permanent change or one simply lasting through the month of October. "Our last wish would be to add to the distress when our goal is to reduce suffering," Ingrid said, noting PETA would continue to distribute literature and use nudity as a promotional tactic.

11

THE OVERTON WINDOW

In 2002, PETA sponsored Gary Yourofsky's lecture tour, according to an interview he did with the *Animal Rights Zone* website. Gary, who had previously been imprisoned for raiding a fur farm, received financial support from PETA for some time. "In November of '05 they said that education wasn't effective and stopped funding me," he told *Animal Rights Zone*. "Harsh words were exchanged as I couldn't believe they pulled the plug." (Attempts to interview Gary for this book were unsuccessful.)

In January, *The Topeka Capital-Journal* published a letter from Ingrid, taking umbrage at a columnist's claim that her organization supported political violence. "Maybe one reason it's so offensive to hear People for the Ethical Treatment of Animals 'linked' to terrorists by our detractors is that our staff was there, on the streets of Manhattan, soon after the attack on the World Trade Center," she wrote. "We arrived with fully equipped rescue vans, introduced ourselves to the emergency personnel guarding Ground Zero, and went to work helping reunite bereaved and shell-shocked people with frightened animals—dogs and cats, birds and rabbits, even turtles, locked, without food or water, in structurally unsound blocks of apartments in the 'hot zone.'"

In the same letter, Ingrid referenced PETA's support for Rod Coronado. "[The columnist] could have honestly pointed out that, seven or so years ago, we did provide funds to guarantee legal representation to a Native American activist," she wrote. "That young man was accused of destroying a laboratory used to study diseases plaguing farms where minks are farmed for fashion. We have no sympathy for those who torment and then painfully anally electrocute animals so that someone in New York can parade about in skins, but we do believe everyone has the right to state their case in court."

Later that month, *The Washington Post* ran a story about a decision by the District of Columbia to halt the use of stray animals as blood donors. Ingrid argued the Washington Humane Society—where she worked previously—should continue to provide strays for this purpose while being more transparent about the policy. "That would be more sensible and ethical than just a knee-jerk reaction of cutting off the use of animals under humane circumstances for blood donation," she said. "The District's obligation is not to outthink the Humane Society about what is humane, but to make sure citizens are properly served and informed."

According to a February piece in *The Fort Wayne Journal Gazette*, Ingrid was happy to see hunters protest an advertisement in which Jeep owners saved deer from blood-sport participants. "Hunters drew more attention to it from their insecurity than Jeep would have ever got on their own," she said. "I think the hunters shot themselves in the foot." No doubt thinking of her own publicity efforts, Ingrid wondered if Jeep's parent company meant to spark outrage with the advertisement. "The fact that they chose it, did it, ran it and got all that attention for it, I think, worked very well for them," she said. "Maybe (DaimlerChrysler) did what any company with good advertising practices do—get the best of both worlds."

The Alamogordo Daily News printed an Associated Press report in early March, in which Ingrid responded to a congressman's demand for further information about PETA providing $1,500 to the Earth Liberation Front. "We don't fund anything illegal and we certainly don't fund the destruction of people's property," she said. "They are taking advantage of people's fears about Sept. 11 to further their own ranching and political interests." The same day, *The New York Times* published an Associated Press brief, regarding a business group's call for PETA to lose its tax-exempt status, due to its association with illegal activism.

In April, *The Whitehorse Star* published a letter from Ingrid, highlighting the connection between violence against animals and violence against humans. "Visiting Canada last week, I was horrified by the story of the gruesome deaths of a string of 'lost' women who are believed to have been murdered by a pig farmer," she wrote, apparently referring to Robert Pickton. "It is now well-established that those who commit acts of violence against human beings 'practice' on animals first. This has been shown to be true of every boy involved in recent school shooting sprees and most, if not all, serial killers."

The Los Angeles Times website included a March article from The Associated Press, covering PETA's attempt to remove polar bears from a Puerto Rican circus. "According to PETA, the U.S. Department of Agriculture should have confiscated the bears when it learned they were kept without air conditioning and swimming pools, which U.S. law requires," journalist Katy Daigle wrote. "The animal-rights group argues the U.S. Fish and Wildlife Service shouldn't have issued the import permit allowing the circus to bring the arctic bears from Canada." The bears were removed that year, according to the organizational chronology on PETA's website.

In November, *The Edinburgh Evening News* printed a brief about a PETA protest in the Scottish capital. "A six-foot 'fish' walked along Princes Street today as part of a campaign to persuade people to turn vegetarian," the unsigned brief stated. "The eye-catching protester was also handing out leaflets encouraging people to give up meat and fish and claiming that the fishing industry is cruel." As she often did, Ingrid used a pun to explain the effort. "The commercial fishing industry sucks the life out of the seas," she said. "We offer a free vegetarian starter kit to get people hooked on compassion."

Later that month, Ingrid revealed another side of herself in a *Washington Post* article about the history of teddy bears. "At age 53, she takes [her childhood toys] Bruno, Rupert Bear and Anonymous—all wearing outfits her mother hand-tailored for them—all over the world with her," journalist Don Oldenburg wrote. PETA's co-founder had a sense of humor about this. "Pretty pathetic, yes?" she said. "They all looked after me, and I looked after them."

Ingrid pushed back against a claim that animals didn't use language, in a letter published by *The Guardian* in December. "It wasn't until about ten years ago that we discovered elephants communicate sub-sonically, again at frequencies we do not hear, as do mice," she wrote "Rhinoceroses are now known to use a language that consists of breathing patterns. And so it goes. The only characteristic that may end up differentiating our species from those we hunt, cage in the circus and experiment upon, is grandiosity."

In January of 2003, *The Indiana Gazette* ran an Associated Press piece, regarding PETA's decision to cancel advertisements featuring the Environmental Protection Agency administrator's dog. "The Scottish terrier, Coors, was to be pictured on billboards by the People for the Ethical Treatment of Animals to protest the agency's use of animals to test the toxicity of certain chemicals," the unsigned article stated. "PETA canceled the campaign after EPA administrator Christie Whitman notified the Norfolk, Virginia-based group that Coors had been euthanized because she was suffering from cancer and was not responding to treatment." Ingrid wrote Whitman a condolence letter.

Ingrid sent a letter to Palestinian leader Yasser Arafat in February, that was reproduced in the second volume of Rabbi Joseph Telushkin's book series, *A Code of Jewish Ethics*. "We have received many calls and letters from people shocked at the bombing in Jerusalem on January 26 in which a donkey, laden with explosives, was intentionally blown up," PETA's co-founder wrote. "All nations behave abominably in many ways when they are fighting their enemies, and animals are always caught in the crossfire. Will you please add to your burdens my request that you appeal to all those who listen to you to leave the animals out of this conflict? We send you our sincere wishes of peace."

In March, *The Guardian* posted an article about a PETA campaign and exhibit, entitled *The Holocaust on Your Plate*. "[It] juxtaposes harrowing images of people in concentration camps with disturbing pictures of animals on farms," journalist David Teather wrote. "One photograph showing an emaciated man is next to another of a starving cow. Another shows a pile of naked human bodies, next to a shot of a heap of pig carcasses." Predictably, this created significant outrage, including a protest from the national director of the Anti-Defamation League.

The Guardian piece quoted a PETA representative, whose family members died in the Holocaust, explaining the rationale behind the campaign. "The very same mindset that made the Holocaust possible—that we can do anything we want to those we decide are 'different or inferior'—is what allows us to commit atrocities against animals every single day," Matt Prescott said. "The fact is, all animals feel pain, fear, and loneliness." (Attempts to interview Matt for this book were unsuccessful.)

In April, *The New Yorker* published a long profile of Ingrid—previously referenced in this book—that included many interesting details. Among these, readers got a sense of the way in which PETA's co-founder approached interviews. "Well, you know, that Reuters reporter was so thrilled when I told him my position on hoof-and-mouth disease," she told journalist Michael Specter, referring to her belief that the economic impact of the illness helped animals. "Don't you need something like that, too?"

The New Yorker piece also revealed Ingrid's will, a particularly morbid publicity stunt. While she left the final decision up to PETA, Ingrid suggested the meat of her body be used in a human barbecue, "to remind the world that the meat of a corpse is all flesh, regardless of whether it comes from a human being or another animal." She asked that her skin be turned into leather products, "to remind the world that human skin and the skin of other animals is the same." She continued, divvying up each part of her body—down to her accusatory pointer finger, which she requested be delivered to the owner of Ringling Brothers.

In a May press release on PETA UK's website, Ingrid linked viruses in the news to meat consumption. "The battle against avian flu, SARS and other diseases begin with your fork," she said. "Rejecting meat means rejecting filthy animal farming practices that cause outbreaks of influenza and avoiding the heart attacks, cancer and strokes that plague meat-eaters."

PETA pledged to halt its campaign against KFC for 60 days, after the fast-food giant agreed to strengthen its animal-welfare requirements, according to a story printed by *The Guardian* later that month. "The company's chickens will get more living space, and 'distractions' and perches, and their slaughter will be more humane," reporter Duncan Campbell wrote, adding KFC would install cameras in its slaughterhouses. Ingrid made clear that she saw this as a first step. "They've got to meet all our demands—which are supported by their own advisers and are the barest of bare minimums where farmed animal welfare is concerned—before we can call off our campaign," PETA's co-founder said.

Later that month, *The New York Post* ran a piece about an advertisement campaign from the Center for Consumer Freedom, linking PETA to underground groups like the Animal Liberation Front and the Earth Liberation Front. "The CCF will broadcast its accusations nationally, beginning with an ad that will air on Fox News Channel today, followed by spots on CNN and MSNBC throughout the week," journalist Richard Johnson wrote.

In the same *New York Post* piece, Ingrid attacked the CCF. "This is a front group for Philip Morris, several logging companies out West, as well as Outback Steakhouse," she was quoted as saying, before focusing her attention on the center's founder, Rick Berman. "He goes around founding these groups and makes a great deal of money from them. All he and his wife do is look at our tax returns and twist things around." Ingrid continued, dismissing the man as a reactionary. "The companies Rick Berman works for kill people every day," she said. "He fought against lowering the alcohol level for drunk driving. He preys on people's fears that the world is about to change."

In July, *The Washington Post* printed an article in which Ingrid claimed actor Jason Alexander was fired as KFC pitchman after questioning animal-welfare standards at PETA's behest. "He said that he wanted to work for an ethical company and that the information we presented was troubling to him," she said. "He called the company's president for us and helped set up a meeting. I believe he was advocating for us." KFC denied it parted ways with Alexander due to disagreements over animal welfare, while Alexander didn't comment on the claim.

PETA sued KFC, according to a story published that same month by *The Louisville Courier-Journal*. "PETA alleged that KFC and Yum violated California's unfair-competition law and its Business and Professions Code by misleading the public about its animal-welfare practices," reporter Patrick Howington wrote. "The suit asked for an injunction blocking KFC and Yum from disseminating false or deceptive information." A PETA representative told Howington the legal action was indirectly related to KFC's failure to live up to its promises—such as installing slaughterhouse cameras.

In September, *The New York Times* ran a piece, in which Ingrid dispatched with the notion that foie-gras production was somehow akin to natural processes. "Migratory fat bears no resemblance whatsoever to ramming a pipe down ducks' necks, pumping pounds of corn mash down their gullets and distending their livers," she said to journalist Patricia Leigh Brown. "These geese and ducks can't fly up the garden path, let alone migrate."

In December, a brief appeared in *The New York Post*, about a letter Ingrid sent to conservative radio host Rush Limbaugh, who was recovering from an addiction to painkillers. Acknowledging he had regularly attacked her on his show, PETA's co-founder—presumably with tongue in cheek—asked Limbaugh to join the fight against animal experimentation. "Researchers are still addicting baboons and other monkeys to drugs under the absurd premise that such studies could help us deal with addiction in humans," she wrote. "You now know from personal experience, having been through detox at least twice, that this doesn't work."

Around 2003, PETA allegedly tried to pass off a report about forced molting, written by Karen Davis, as its own. "I had researched, written and published this paper, pulling together all of this information that I had gotten," she told this writer, noting some of her source documents came from a Freedom of Information Act request. "I spent a decade and a half—at least—just on this topic. I knew it backward and forward and still do. Then along comes PETA." Bob Chorush, one of Ingrid's subordinates, sent Karen a draft of the organization's report on the subject, which was blatantly plagiarized. "It was my own document," Karen said. "All they did was tweak a couple of phrases and words here and there."

In an interview with this writer, Karen claimed Bob, who has since died of pancreatic cancer, told her Ingrid approved of the plagiarism herself. "I don't know what Ingrid was thinking," Karen said. "But that's what she did." Karen contacted Ingrid by phone or email, seeking to prevent the report from being distributed in PETA's name. "I don't remember that she gave a damn," Karen said. "They never used it. I told her that was prohibited—that this was mine and this belonged to United Poultry Concerns."

While not addressing plagiarism specifically, Matt Ball said it wasn't unusual for large animal organizations to take credit for the work of smaller groups. "I was involved with the Animal Rights

Community of Greater Cincinnati," he told this author. "We were always doing demos against Procter & Gamble. We couldn't get media in Cincinnati. So when we decided we were finally going to get arrested—to try to break through the stranglehold that Procter & Gamble have had on media coverage—In Defense of Animals took basically full credit for that. They made it sound like they were doing all of it. That's pretty common."

In February of 2004, *The New York Post* printed an article, in which Ingrid condemned Vice President Dick Cheney, who had apparently taken part in a canned hunt. "You can't get any lower than shooting ducks in a barrel," she was quoted as saying. "Here's a man who's come close to death with a heart attack, and yet it has not dawned on him that all creatures value their lives."

PETA sent a condolence to President George W. Bush, following the death of his dog—according to an Associated Press report, published by *The Winchester Star* later that month. "The English Springer Spaniel was put down Saturday at a veterinarian's recommendation after she suffered a series of strokes, including one last week," the unsigned article stated. "She was 14 years old." PETA argued the president's choice would provide a good example for Americans. "The number one problem for the best-kept dogs is that their people cannot bring themselves to say goodbye long after the animals' joy in living has left due to illness," Ingrid said.

In April, *The Edmonton Journal* printed a letter from Ingrid, defending a PETA advertisement referencing a Canadian serial killer. "Our ad is a simple, forthright plea for compassion at a time when we're all reeling from the shock of Robert Pickton's alleged crimes," she wrote. "Shouldn't we all say, loud and clear: It is needless, wrong and indulgent to hurt and kill others, regardless of age, race, gender or species? Most of us can't stop serial killers, but we can take small steps every day to reduce suffering and killing simply by choosing not to eat the corpses of animals. Fortunately, many people did understand what we are trying to accomplish."

Demonstrating the sometimes-surprising degree to which she was willing to work within the confines of existing animal exploitation, Ingrid asked the National Rifle Association to teach seal hunters—who traditionally killed their prey with bludgeons—how to use guns, according to an article published that month by *The Washington Post*. "In this age of sophisticated weaponry, many are still crudely killed with primitive cudgels," she wrote in a letter to NRA president Kayne Robinson. "Won't you stand with us in seeking a quick kill?"

A few days after, *The Janesville Gazette* ran a piece, apparently taken from wire services, in which Ingrid described a phone call from a man identifying himself as Mathew Knowles, father, and manager to singer Beyoncé Knowles. PETA had protested the pop star for wearing fur. "I wasn't in, but he left a message, 'Tell her we're going to get to know each other very, very well,'" Ingrid said. "You could take that as a good sign—if you're Julie Andrews. If, however, you're a realist, you look for a subpoena." She added the caller identification traced back to Sony, Beyoncé's label.

Still in April, *The Florida Times-Union* covered a rally against Yerkes National Primate Research Center. "They are nothing more than concentration camps for animals," Ingrid said, addressing the crowd. "At least once a year, someone should remind the community that what goes on [at Yerkes] is not civilized." She continued, describing vivisection as a retrograde practice. "Science is supposed to be about innovation," PETA's co-founder said. "But they're doing the same things they were doing to animals 200 years ago."

News outlets across the country received flesh burgers as part of a promotional campaign for the stoner comedy *Harold and Kumar Go to Whitecastle*, according to a May article in *The New York Daily News*. Ingrid was quoted—though it wasn't clear if she was referring to the film itself, the promotional campaign, or both. "They can't say that no animals were harmed to make this movie," she told journalist Lloyd Grove. "It sounds like it could be disconcerting and rather sad and bloody. This is the new PG-13: 'Pathetic,' 'Gross' and '13 kinds of gut bacteria.'"

Later that month, *The Melbourne Herald Sun* reported Ingrid's organization was threatening to push for a boycott of Australian wool. "PETA is outraged 2,000 sheep died of hypothermia in a cold snap in East Gippsland last week shortly after being shorn of their protective wool," journalist Sam Edmund wrote. "PETA was also a vocal opponent of Australia's treatment of the 50,000 sheep shipped to the Middle East aboard the *Cormo Express* last year." Ingrid argued nothing was being done to protect the animals. "From the outback to the clothes rack, sheep raised for wool live miserable lives and die bloody deaths at the hands of Australians," she said. "The Australian Government is yet to lift a finger to curb even the worst abuses."

In a late-May press release, on the PETA UK website, Ingrid advocated for more vegan-friendly vehicles. "DaimlerChrysler could take a truly classy stand—instead of contributing to the slaughter of thousands of cows—by offering alternatives to cow skin in all its cars," she said. "Many wealthy consumers find nothing luxurious about smelly, creaky preserved hides and want Mercedes to market luxury cars that don't come equipped with misery." Why Ingrid seemed to be focused on vehicles marketed to the rich is unclear. Perhaps she believed changes made in such cars would influence the broader industry.

In June, Wayne Pacelle became president of the Humane Society of the United States and began steering the organization leftward. In an interview recorded prior to Wayne's resignation amidst sexual misconduct allegations, Peter Singer argued Wayne's ascension to leadership of the traditionally-conservative group would not have been possible without Ingrid's work, moving the Overton window. "Many larger societies, but HSUS would be the best example, were pushed to go in a more progressive direction by the fact that they could see PETA was growing so fast and getting so much support— therefore undercutting their membership base and their donor base," the philosopher said. "They realized that they had to try to appeal to some of these people to overcome that."

That same month, *The Los Angeles Times* ran a story about a two-day PETA conference held at a high school, where Ingrid spoke. "I think the animal protection movement is a sleeping giant," she said. "The same way young people brought their parents along to environmentalism, they'll bring their parents along with animal rights." The establishment of underground groups was inevitable. "It's like any social justice movement," Newkirk said. "It was true with the suffragettes. You have people who write letters and teach the public and you have people who are more militant and don't have the patience to wait ten or twenty years for change."

According to an August brief in *The Logansport Pharos-Tribune*, Ingrid wrote a letter to former First Lady Nancy Reagan, informing her PETA planned to use her husband's photograph in a campaign linking the consumption of animal fats to an increased risk of developing Alzheimer's. The former president, who suffered from the disease, had recently died. "We hope that you will be happy that we chose your husband's powerful image," Ingrid wrote. "This campaign would be helped significantly by a brief note of support from you." A representative for the Reagan family sent PETA a cease-and-desist letter in response.

In November, *The Australian* printed a message from Ingrid, calling for reform. "Sloppy sheep farmers should not be permitted to pull the wool over people's eyes when it comes to whether or not viable alternatives to mulesing exist," she wrote. "Good animal husbandry practices, such as monitoring for fly-strike and shearing sheep backsides at the right time, have been tossed aside in favor of crude and cruel mulesing, a procedure that one veterinarian describes as flaying lamb's rump flesh."

In the same message, Ingrid chalked up continued use of the procedure to miserliness. "Stud owners say that abandoning mulesing would mean—heaven forbid—that farmers would have to check the sheep almost daily," she wrote. "They also say that if farmers had to shear the hindquarters of sheep four times a year instead of once or not at all, it would involve having to use extra employees. Cheap is the word, but not in the shops, where the price tags on sweaters and blankets show no signs of these cruelly cut corners."

PETA had apparently begun its boycott, as the Australian Associated Press posted a story in December about an industry group seeking help from the legal system to stop the campaign. "[Australian Wool Innovation] is trying to use the Trade Practices Act in its injunction," the unsigned article stated, "although there are doubts over how this will apply to PETA's actions in the United States where retailer Abercrombie and Fitch has stopped selling Australian wool products." Ingrid was undeterred. "I remain extremely confident that AWI's claims will fail," she said. "No-one has the right to prevent consumers and retailers from hearing the facts about the cruel treatment of sheep by the Australian wool industry."

Following a seven-week undercover investigation, PETA demanded the prosecution of a kosher slaughterhouse, according to an Associated Press article, printed by *The Ottumwa Courier* in December. The animal organization alleged the facility violated state law, which mandated 'humane' methods of killing. "Again and again, when we pull back the curtain on slaughterhouses and factory farms, we find a level of abuse that would make most people lose their lunch," Ingrid said.

12

OLD WOUNDS

Ingrid asked George W. Bush not to wear a beaver-felt cowboy hat to his inauguration, *The Baltimore Sun* reported in January of 2005. "You may not realize that beavers are gentle, family-oriented animals who mate for life, raise their children in loving families and remain lifelong friends with their offspring," PETA's co-founder wrote in a message to the president. "Beavers are even known to enjoy flute music."

Later that month, *The Sydney Sun-Herald* provided an update on the boycott spearheaded by PETA. "It had been only two days since the news had reached Sydney on January 15 that Benetton was reviewing its position as a major buyer of Australian wool," reporter Catharine Munro wrote. "But [Australian ambassador to Italy] Peter Woolcott had already traveled swiftly to the industrial city of Ponzano for a three-hour meeting to talk them around." The fashion company's executives denounced the boycott, but Ingrid was unfazed. "We have always been tenacious and that's our trademark," she said. "We will hang on like pit bulls because we know the sheep can't do it themselves."

In March, *The Saint Joseph News-Press* also covered backlash to the wool boycott. "Eat-A-Sheep-for-PETA-Day is the brainchild of Ian Slack-Smith, a member of Australia's parliament and a former sheep and cattle farmer in New South Wales, who claims that PETA is misinformed about the shipping conditions of the sheep," the unsigned brief stated. Ingrid tried to turn the tables on Slack-Smith, by offering her support to the farcical campaign. "We are all for people getting together to reduce the sum total of sheep suffering, and eating poor old Australian sheep who would otherwise have ended up being marinated in their own waste en route to the Middle East would accomplish that," she said.

After the failure of AWI's court action, Ingrid made an offer to the industry group, according to an Australian Associated Press article posted that month. "PETA and I will waive your reimbursement of our legal costs if you will immediately withdraw your support for mulesing mutilations and live export and urge farmers to move ahead by breeding from bare breech rams, employing good husbandry methods of flystrike control, and slaughtering Australian sheep in Australia," she was quoted as writing. "Publicly, you claim to be concerned about sheep welfare. This proposal provides you with the opportunity to put our money where your mouth is." Unsurprisingly, AWI declined the offer.

In April, PETCO issued a press release on its website, announcing an agreement between the company and PETA. "PETCO will end the sale of large birds in the company's stores," the release stated. "PETA will end its boycott of PETCO and its protests at the company's stores. In agreeing to end its campaign against PETCO, PETA will take down its 'PETCOCruelty' website, remove all references to 'PETNO' on all sites affiliated with the organization, and withdraw its support of the use of the 'PETNO' logo by other groups." According to the chronology on PETA's website, the organization also secured a commitment from PETCO to make provisions for the rodents in its possession.

Ingrid clarified PETA's position on working dogs in a letter published by *The Sunday Tasmanian* in May. "We support hearing ear dogs because they are rescued from pounds and shelters and are not kept in harnesses or forbidden to socialize," she wrote, "They have meaningful, interesting lives. On the other hand, guide dogs for the blind are bred even though millions of dogs are euthanized every year because of overpopulation and are substitutes or fob offs for a society that doesn't wish to expend more funds and reach out to the blind in a meaningful way."

PETA conducted an undercover investigation into Covance, a contract research company, according to a media statement issued later that month, archived on the website of PETA UK. "The tape shows experimenters using their power over the monkeys to torture and torment them while lab supervisors stand by or even join in," Ingrid said. "The US Department of Agriculture is empowered to stop this type of abuse, yet its inspectors only enter these monkey prisons once a year, and everyone at the labs knows which day that is."

The Jacksonville Daily News printed an Associated Press report in June, detailing a case in which two PETA workers faced charges of felony animal cruelty. They had been found dumping the corpses of dogs and cats in a shopping center garbage. "It's hideous," Ingrid said. "I think this is so shocking it's bound to hurt our work." She claimed the workers had been tasked with bringing the animals back to headquarters, where they would be put to death. However, that wasn't what the veterinarians who gave the animals to PETA had been told. "These were just kittens we were trying to find homes for," one such professional said. "PETA said they would do that, but these cats never made it out of the county."

In July, *The Florida Times-Union* ran a story about PETA's Running of the Nudes, which, as its name suggested, was a clothing-optional protest in Spain of the Running of the Bulls. "Tormenting and butchering animals for entertainment is something straight out of the Dark Ages," Ingrid said. "Tourists flocking to Pamplona are looking for a thrill and our Running of the Nudes aims to give them just that without harming a hair on a bull's back."

In August, *The Sedalia Democrat* published a letter, in which Ingrid wrote in favor of stem-cell research, arguing it would lessen the use of animals in vivisection. "I join Senator Bill Frist in his support of the use of embryonic stem cells for research that may lead to treatments and cures for Alzheimer's disease and other ailments," she said. "It may not have occurred to many people, but the failure to use stem cells also means that more animals are hurt and killed in substandard experiments."

The Baltimore Sun printed a piece on in-vitro meat later that month. "Progress in this area is welcome for anyone who has any compassion for animals at all," Ingrid told reporter Mariana Minaya. "The list of good this will do is enormous." She was confident there was a market for the product. "Look at the fact that ten years ago, no one had even heard of soy milk except in a commune in Berkeley, and today it's in every major supermarket," PETA's co-founder said. "We don't know how quickly things will catch on. I'm sure they can give you a cloned meat with all the texture and taste you desire and maybe more."

While acknowledging the pain it created, Ingrid defended a PETA exhibit comparing human slavery to animal agriculture, according to an Associated Press article, published by *The Harrisonburg Daily News-Record* in September. "I unequivocally apologize for the hurt and upset that this exhibit has caused some of its viewers," she said. "I realize that old wounds can be slow to heal and for not helping them heal, I am also sorry. That said, I would fail in my duty if I allowed this exhibit to disappear." One of the exhibit panels featured a photograph of a human lynching beside an image of a cow hanging in a slaughterhouse.

Carol Adams slammed PETA's exhibit. "They were exploiting the exploitation of African Americans," she told this writer. "The kind of theory I write says that we can't substitute one oppression for another. The oppressions are interconnected. But they're not parallel. They're not interchangeable. What these campaigns do— from PETA—is they erode the specifics. Where's white supremacy? What's the role of white supremacy in furthering meat-eating?"

Amie 'Breeze' Harper struck a similar note in *Sistah Vegan*, a book she edited. "Even though I am an animal-rights supporter, I feel that PETA's campaign strategies often fail to give a historical context for why they use certain images that are connected to a painful history of racially motivated violence against particular, nonwhite racialized humans," Amie wrote. "The PETA exhibit and the ensuing controversy were handled insensitively." (Attempts to interview her for this book were unsuccessful.)

Speaking with this author, Jane Velez-Mitchell insisted outrage surrounding PETA's Holocaust on Your Plate campaign and slavery exhibit was rooted in speciesism. "We have so demonized animals that to compare humans—in any way, shape or form—with animals is deemed an insult," she said. "To compare something horrible and horrific that happened to humans with something horrible and horrific happening to animals does not diminish humans. It's just an example of how we're so brainwashed as a culture."

After reaching a deal with the Australian Wool Growers Association, PETA announced a 45-day moratorium on its boycotting campaign.

But that was ending, according to a September story posted by the Australian Associated Press. Ingrid promised to resume her efforts if AWI and Wool Producers didn't agree to phase out mulesing and improve the welfare of animals shipped abroad. "Change is inevitable, so AWI and other foot-draggers are not just hurting the sheep, they're also hurting themselves," she said. "We're prepared to re-launch a vigorous campaign against the Australian wool industry if that's the only way to reduce the suffering of Australian sheep."

In October, *Satya Magazine* ran a piece by Ingrid, listing ways in which the government kept tabs on her organization. "This summer, PETA emerged from a politically motivated twenty-month IRS audit, a desperate fishing expedition to try to find anything that might justify the removal of our tax-exempt status," she wrote. "Our mail continues to be opened by the U.S. Postal Service, which denies this when served with Freedom of Information requests, yet does not explain why our mail often arrives at its destination inside USPS envelopes."

That same month, The Australian Associated Press reported that PETA planned to stage a demonstration outside of Australia's embassy to the United States. "Campaigners will target the embassy with posters of bloody sheep and will burn a giant Australian five dollar note as part of its protest," the unsigned brief stated. "PETA says the protest is one of many similar rallies taking place around the world." Ingrid suggested mulesing would turn off shoppers. "The Australian government's position that sheep and lambs are commodities and that it can do what it wants to them shames Australia in the eyes of a world where animal welfare is a very real issue for consumers," she said.

In December, following the theatrical release of *The Chronicles of Narnia, The Frederick News-Post* ran a column, in which Ingrid argued author C.S. Lewis would embrace animal rights if he were alive. "It's true that Lewis' strong faith shines through in the pages of the book, but something else does too: Lewis' fervent belief that animals should be treated well and his outrage when animals are killed," Ingrid wrote, adding Lewis' views were also made clear in his nonfiction. "Lewis abhorred abuse of animals and condemned even the cruelty that was sanctioned by educated men in authority—experimentation on animals."

AWI was considering an alternative to mulesing, according to a piece published by *The Sydney Morning Herald* in January of 2006. The alternative seems to have involved cutting off an animal's circulation until a patch of skin withered. Unimpressed, Ingrid asked AWI's chairman an Australia's agricultural minister to "apply the clips to your own backsides in the same way that they would be applied to a lamb and then leave them there for a week, at the end of which you will each submit to a medical exam. If the examining physician declares that you have suffered no pain, we'll announce our endorsement right away."

The New York Times printed an article in March, detailing how plant-managers at the aforementioned kosher slaughterhouse gave gifts of meat to Agriculture Department inspectors. "Also, some of the plant's ten inspectors made faulty inspections of carcasses, failed to correct unsanitary conditions and were seen sleeping and playing computer games on the job, said the report, by the agency's inspector general," journalist Donald G. McNeil Jr. wrote. Ingrid demanded action. "[The Agriculture Department] should fire all the inspectors who accepted gifts and did nothing about these egregious abuses of the animals whom they are supposed to protect," she said.

In April, *The Times of India* covered some nonhuman activism in that country. "Disguised as bears and waving a sign that reads 'Save My Skin', Swati Shah and Roni of People for the Ethical Treatment of Animals (PETA) India are following Prince Charles around to encourage him to convince his mother Queen Elizabeth II to call off the slaughter of Canada's black bears for the ceremonial bearskin hats that her guards wear and use faux fur instead," reporter Amit Banerjee stated.

Ingrid was quoted, speaking on behalf of the satellite organization in the same *Times of India* piece. "Prince Charles is known to be a staunch defender of the environment, so it would make sense for him to oppose the slaughter of black bears for something as frivolous as a ceremonial hat," she said. "Until he comes to his senses, the PETA bear will be a regular fixture at Charles' public events in Britain and overseas and will not go away until these bearskin hats become extinct."

In April, PETA issued a press release, celebrating a unanimous ruling by New York Appellate Court justices to uphold a felony conviction against someone who stomped a goldfish to death. "We commend the entire judicial panel for its landmark effort to afford fish—whose suffering and abuse have historically been ignored—the same legal protections that all animals deserve," Ingrid said. "It is our hope that this ruling will send a message to would-be animal abusers that cruelty to any animal, no matter how small or misunderstood, will be taken seriously."

Following negotiations with PETA, Polo Ralph Lauren agreed to stop using fur in its apparel and home collections, according to an Associated Press report, published in June by *The Wisconsin State Journal*. Ingrid praised the move. "Ralph Lauren clothes have always been elegant, but now you can feel comfortable inside and out knowing that the company has made this compassionate decision," she said.

In August, *The Wisconsin State Journal* ran an Associated Press piece about the mass-slaughter of dogs in China, following a rabies outbreak. PETA canceled orders of the group's merchandise that was made in the country. "We are urging everyone to actively boycott—not a word we use lightly—anything from China given the bludgeoning killing of thousands of dogs," Ingrid said. When Beijing adopted a one-dog policy to combat disease, PETA's co-founder reluctantly supported the measure, according to an Associated Press article, printed by *The New York Times* in November.

The New York Post printed an amusing tidbit in September, that demonstrated the degree to which PETA had become notorious in certain industries. "Fashion Week security recognized PETA honchos Dan Matthews and Ingrid Newkirk in the front row (along with Ivana Trump and Illeana Douglas) at the Marc Bouwer show on Friday, whereupon they quickly descended upon the animal-loving duo and tried to eject them from the tents," journalist Danica Lo wrote. "Fortunately, the fur foes were seated next to Bouwer's mother, who assured security that Matthews and Newkirk were guests of Bouwer, who does not use fur and leather in his collections."

In October, *The New York Post* covered a PETA action in France. "Ingrid Newkirk and Dan Mathews and a horde of protesters spent Monday night in a Paris slammer," the unsigned brief stated. "The group was arrested after busting into the Jean Paul Gaultier flagship boutique and dousing the designer's street-level windows with red paint while wearing 'bloodied' donated furs and shouting 'Gaultier! Killer!' for over an hour. Brigitte Bardot defended the protest."

The Elyria Chronicle-Telegram published a column by Ingrid in January of 2007, celebrating the birthday of vegetarian Albert Schweitzer. "Equally important to the poor people he served in equatorial Africa and to the wounded and orphaned animals he took in, from pelicans to pigs to baby gorillas, he worked to stop everyone's pain and suffering," PETA's co-founder wrote. "A dose of Schweitzer's philosophy would do us a world of good in today's complex society."

PETA criticized former vice-president Al Gore, according to a story printed by *The Brisbane Courier-Mail* in March. "The organization, which is known for its often bizarre publicity stunts, yesterday announced it had sent Mr. Gore, pictured, whose global warming documentary *An Inconvenient Truth* won an Oscar last month, a letter accusing him of being a hypocrite for contributing to green-house gases by eating meat," journalist Peta Hellard wrote. "Ingrid Newkirk claimed that studies showed raising animals for food gen-erated more greenhouse gases than all the cars and trucks in the world combined."

In May, *The New York Times* reported on promises PETA secured from the beverage industry. "Under pressure from animal rights advocates, two soft drink giants, Coca-Cola and Pepsi-Co, have agreed to stop directly financing research that uses animals to test or develop their products, except where such testing is required by law," journalist Brenda Goodman wrote. "Roll International, the company that makes Pom Wonderful pomegranate juice, agreed to cease tests on animals after PETA disclosed a 2005 study financed by the company that tested the juice to see if it might relieve artifi-cially induced erectile dysfunction in rabbits."

In June, The Australian Broadcasting Corporation posted an article on its website about an agreement between PETA and AWI. "[AWI chairman] McLachlan says PETA has agreed as part of the deal to stop targeting individual retailers until 2010, when the practice of mulesing will be phased out," the unsigned article stated. "PETA founder Ingrid Newkirk says while the organization will not call for a boycott of specific retailers, it will still urge people not to buy Australian wool."

Ingrid took a Democratic politician to task, in a letter published that July by *The Progress-Index*. "While it's wonderful that Virginia Sen. Jim Webb could welcome his son home from Iraq for Father's Day weekend, it's a shame that he chose to spend their peaceful time together killing small animals with a fishing pole and hook," she wrote. "Studies have shown that fish feel pain, that their mouths are as sensitive as our fingers, that they communicate with one another, and that they even use tools."

In August, *The New York Daily News* reported that Ingrid faxed a message to Karl Rove, attacking the Republican strategist for a planned dove-hunting expedition. "From your frequent hunting trips to your bizarre little rap at the Radio and Television Correspondents' Association dinner [where Rove joked that he liked to 'tear the tops off small animals'], it is clear that you lack the ability to empathize with other living beings," she wrote. "You consistently prove that you care less about animal welfare than Alberto Gonzales cares about habeas corpus." PETA's co-founder recommended that Rove bring along Vice President Dick Cheney, who accidentally shot a friend while hunting.

The Wisconsin State Journal printed a brief later that month, regarding the involvement of Atlanta Falcons quarterback Michael Vick in dogfighting. Ingrid was outraged by actor Jamie Foxx's defense of Vick, which appeared to suggest the blood sport was part of African-American culture. "It is cheap and dirty and wrong to call this a cultural thing unless Foxx believes that cruelty is a black thing—when it isn't," PETA's co-founder was quoted as saying. "It may be his thing, but it is not a black thing."

Ingrid was similarly surprised to hear Whoopi Goldberg defend Vick, according to a September piece in *The New York Daily News*. The actress claimed dogfighting was something of a Southern tradition. "I think a lot of people who live and work in the South—as PETA does—will not appreciate the view that cruelty to dogs is an accepted Southern pastime," Ingrid said. "Those who fight dogs do so in New York, Chicago and even the Republic of Ireland, and what unites them is lawlessness and callousness, not whether they eat grits or Belgian waffles for breakfast."

Vick accepted PETA's invitation to take a course in animal protection, Ingrid wrote in a column published by *The Elyria Chronicle-
Telegram* in October. "After eight hours of watching video footage
in which he saw elephants work cooperatively to rescue a founder-
ing baby elephant from a mud hole and pigs become afraid after
smelling a slaughterhouse passageway, Vick admitted that he had
never considered such things," Ingrid stated. "He ended up sharing
examples from his own life about the loyalty of his aunt's dog and
wondered aloud about how animals must feel when left outside on
a cold wintry night or kept in a barren cage."

Ingrid acknowledged that Vick had nothing to lose. "He presented himself humbly, listened attentively and answered pointed questions, but we are not naive enough to imagine that we know what
goes on in his head and heart," she wrote in *The Elyria Chronicle-
Telegram* column. "He knew that PETA was not offering him a get-
out-of-jail-free card and that our position remains that he must
serve a substantial sentence as a warning to others that money and
stardom will not excuse heinous acts of wanton cruelty."

PETA established a satellite organization in Australia, according to
a November piece by the Australian Associated Press. "One of our
primary campaigns will be to stop the wool industry's mulesing
mutilations of lambs and live export of terrified sheep," Ingrid said.
"But like every other PETA affiliate across the globe, we will also
be attacking animal abuse anywhere and everywhere that we can."

Later that month, *The Walla Walla Union-Bulletin* ran an article from
The Associated Press, regarding a PETA undercover investigation of
the Oregon National Primate Research Center. "These animals live
in terror every second of every day," Ingrid said. "They are shut in
metal boxes and killed for nicotine and alcohol experiments as well
as other wasteful and repetitive studies." PETA claimed the facility
violated animal-welfare laws.

Still in November, *I Am an Animal*, a documentary about Ingrid,
premiered on HBO. Perhaps most notably, the film included rel-
atively-frank assessments of PETA's tactics from other leaders of
the nonhuman movement. "The intention is to get whatever attention they can, by whatever means," said Priscilla Feral, Friends
of Animals president. "Now, that makes you good at fundraising,
perhaps. [But] is that how you get a society to respect animals? I

don't think it does a thing for animals." She went further, arguing PETA exploited racism and sexism.

The leader of the Humane Society of the United States suggested Ingrid's organization was a liability. "There are many times when the opposition hoists up PETA as the norm of animal welfare," Wayne Pacelle said in the HBO documentary. "[The opposition] says, these are the animal-welfare people; these are the things that they do. That can't help." (Attempts to interview Priscilla and Wayne for this book were unsuccessful.)

In December, *The Beckley Register-Herald* ran an Associated Press brief about PETA naming Senator Robert Byrd 'Person of the Year,' due to a speech he made against dogfighting and pro-animal legislation he wrote or supported. "Much animal suffering has been alleviated thanks to Senator Byrd, and this year we are proud to honor him for giving a voice to the voiceless," Ingrid said. If she sought to disprove allegations that outrage to Vick's behavior had racial undertones, singling out Byrd's comments on the issue for praise seemed like a remarkably poor choice, given he was a former Ku Klux Klan leader who filibustered the 1964 Civil Rights Act.

13

A $1 MILLION PRIZE

According to the chronology on PETA's website, the organization convinced Safeway, Harris Teeter, and a Canadian KFC buyer to make animal-welfare improvements in 2008. That February, *The Virginian-Pilot* covered PETA's campaign targeting Harris Teeter. "The Charlotte, North Carolina-based grocery company will offer a new line of cage-free eggs and buy more chicken and pork products from suppliers who also are animal-friendly," reporter Debbie Messina wrote. "PETA officials had planned to appeal to Harris Teeter shareholders at the company's annual meeting Thursday to step up animal welfare policies. Matt Prescott, PETA spokesman, said Harris Teeter's plans are 'groundbreaking,' therefore, there was no longer a need to address shareholders."

Ingrid was arrested in India, according to an article from the Indo-Asian News Service, published in January by *The Hindustan Times*. "Coimbatore police have booked People for Ethical Treatment of Animals (PETA) chief Ingrid Newkirk for attempting to blindfold a statue of Mahatma Gandhi in the city in protest against the apex court allowing jallikattu," the unsigned article stated. "PETA legal affairs coordinator N.G. Jayasimha has also been booked for helping Newkirk. The PETA activists have said they were only trying to draw attention to the fact that cruelty to animals and events like jallikattu should not happen in the land of Gandhi."

In February, United Press International reported Fox turned down two advertisements targeting KFC that PETA sought to air during the Super Bowl. Explaining the decision, Fox cited its policy of not running advocacy spots. Ingrid pointed out the hypocrisy of this stance. "It's ridiculous that the network has no objection to ads that advocate killing animals and eating them," she said. "But it won't give a paid ad with a humane message equal time."

Later that month, The Australian Associated Press covered PETA's ongoing efforts to reform the wool industry. "One of the world's largest clothing retailers has slapped a ban on Australian wool after pressure from a US animal rights group," journalist Peter Mitchell wrote. "Sweden-based H&M, with 1,500 stores in 28 countries, will source wool from nations other than Australia after the People for the Ethical Treatment of Animals (PETA) complained the Australian wool industry had 'reneged' on a promise to phase out mulesing sheep by 2010."

Ingrid was quoted in the same article, praising the move. "We commend H&M for adding its name to the growing worldwide effort to stop mulesing," she said. "The company's decision will hasten the day when the Australian wool industry is seen as nothing more than lamb mutilators and sheep abusers."

In March, *The New York Times* printed a piece, focusing on the debate within the nonhuman movement about what to do with animals rescued from Vick's dogfighting operation. Ingrid opposed sending the canines to Best Friends Animal Sanctuary, which she called 'an expensive Camelot.' Rather, PETA argued the animals should be put to death, and funds allocated for their care should be used in other ways. "These are celebrity dogs," Ingrid told journalist William C. Rhoden. "That isn't a good use of money, it isn't the best use of time. The Vick dogs are the least likely candidates for success."

Michael Mountain—co-founder of Best Friends Animal Sanctuary—was quoted in the same *New York Times* piece, slamming Ingrid's organization. "I don't think PETA's argument is with us, I think it's with themselves," he said Rhoden. "It's really difficult as an animal-rights, animal-protection, animal-whatever-you-want-to-call-it organization to explain away the fact that pretty much all the animals you rescue, you kill. It doesn't make logical sense; it doesn't make emotional sense."

Ingrid opposed a Wales badger cull in an April letter printed by *Wales on Sunday*. "The plan to kill badgers to supposedly stop the spread of tuberculosis in cattle is a cruel and misguided attempt to place the blame for TB in cattle somewhere other than where it belongs—in my view, with the meat and dairy industries," she wrote. "Science shows that slaughtering badgers doesn't control tuberculosis but actually causes it to spread in a 'ripple effect'—infected badgers disperse and carry the infection to a larger range."

Later that month, *The New York Times* published an article about PETA offering a $1 million prize to the first person who established a commercially-viable means of creating in-vitro meat—by 2012. "A founder of PETA, Ingrid Newkirk, said she had been hoping to get the organization involved in advancing in vitro meat technology for at least a decade," reporter John Schwartz wrote. "But, Ms. Newkirk said, the decision to sponsor a prize caused 'a near civil war in our office,' since so many PETA members are repulsed by the thought of eating animal tissue, even if no animals are killed."

Lisa Lange, PETA's vice president, explained her objection to in-vitro meat in the April *New York Times* article. "My main concern is, as the largest animal rights organization in the world, it's our job to introduce the philosophy and hammer it home that animals are not ours to eat," Lisa told Schwartz. "I remember saying I would be much more comfortable promoting eating roadkill." Thankfully, Ingrid's forward-thinking pragmatism won out, although the 2012 deadline—later extended to 2014—meant no one claimed the prize. (Attempts to interview Lisa for this book were unsuccessful.)

PETA defended itself to the Advertising Standards Authority, which had received a complaint saying the group's anti-KFC leaflet was offensive, according to a press release distributed later that month, archived on the website of PETA UK. "As an animal protection group, it is our duty to share uncomfortable information about animal abuse with the buying public," Ingrid was quoted as writing. "Faulting PETA for giving people a glimpse into how chickens end up in the KFC bucket or box would be like faulting the police for showing people how to spot a fraud."

Following the death of a racehorse in competition, Ingrid slammed presidential candidate Hillary Clinton for having urged people to bet on the animal, according to a May piece in *The New York Times*. "She's partly culpable because it's money that makes them race, and money that makes them race prematurely," Ingrid said. "It was inappropriate." She continued, explaining PETA's goal was to stigmatize the racing industry. "If we suddenly make it kind of tainted, it will not be really the place where you want to be seen," Ingrid said. "We want other politicians, other people, not to wish to be associated with it."

In June, *The Newcastle-upon-Tyne Evening Chronicle* published a story about PETA's opposition to the use of animals in education. "St. Agnes RC Primary School in Ryton, Gateshead, adopted some racing pigeons from a nearby loft to help improve pupils' math and literacy skills," the unsigned story stated. "Teachers said the birds were used in classes studying flight paths, plotting wind speeds, checking race progress and looking at geography." Ingrid criticized this. "Animals should not be seen as disposable learning tools but as fascinating beings who have their own natural way of living," she said. "They do not want to be handled and banded, and they do not relish long, arduous and even hazardous journeys back to a cage or loft."

When a hotelier died, leaving instructions that her estimated $8-billion fortune be put toward the welfare of dogs, PETA and HSUS sought a portion of the funds. Apparently, Ingrid wanted to use the money on spay-and-neuter programs. "Many people cannot afford the surgery for their dogs," she was quoted as saying in a July piece in *The Cranbrook Daily Townsman.* "In these hard times, with house foreclosures, and people trying to pay for food and fuel, the last thing they're going to think about is the care and sterilization of dogs." Ingrid noted one of the estate's trustees was a PETA donor.

The New York Times ran an article later that month, reporting on a bill in the Spanish Parliament, which would reform how the country treated humanity's closest relatives. "If the bill passes—the news agency Reuters predicts it will—it would become illegal in Spain to kill apes except in self-defense," journalist Donald G. McNeill Jr. wrote. "Torture, including in medical experiments, and arbitrary imprisonment, including for circuses or films, would be forbidden." Ingrid praised the bill, calling it "a great start at breaking down the species barriers, under which humans are regarded as godlike and the rest of the animal kingdom, whether chimpanzees or clams, are treated like dirt."

Still in July, *The Los Angeles Times* published a profile of Wayne—for which Ingrid was interviewed. "He's a very charming man, and that never hurts," PETA's co-founder said. "I'm a rather abrasive sort." However, she wasn't without criticism of the HSUS leader, who she had known for twenty years. "I am keen that he really go after the pet food manufacturers who still test on animals," Ingrid said. "Wayne has a slower approach."

After a man named Tim McLean was murdered and cannibalized, PETA attempted to place an advertisement linking the incident to consumption of animal flesh. Ingrid defended her organization's choice in an August letter printed in *The Swan Valley Star and Times*. "The details of this incomprehensible murder were sickening to everyone, and our hearts go out to Tim McLean's family and the witnesses," she wrote. "We must ask people to realize that when they buy meat, they are paying someone—for the sake of a sandwich—to do exactly what was done to Tim McLean. Of course, such comparisons are uncomfortable and irritating, but they're not inaccurate."

In October, PETA posted a blog entry on its website, celebrating 22 criminal charges which resulted from the organization's investigation of a pig farm. "This is a small victory for farmed animals, but we mustn't forget that Hormel, which financially supports this farm, has by all appearances yet to make any changes because of this investigation," Christine Doré wrote. "It has refused to meet with us or even watch all of the footage, which we have repeatedly offered to show the company. Maybe now that the law has spoken up, Hormel will finally listen."

When Barack Obama said he would bring a dog to the White House, Ingrid urged the president-elect to adopt a shelter animal. "No one needs to tell you that this country is proud to be a melting pot and that there is something deeply wrong and elitist about wanting only a purebred dog," PETA's co-founder was quoted as writing in a November article published by *The Chicago Tribune*. Ultimately, however, the Obama family chose a purebred animal.

The Ad Council agreed to stop supporting the use of certain animals in promotions, according to a PETA blog entry posted later that month. "After learning from PETA just how hideous life can be for great apes who are kept captive and forced to perform in advertisements, thanks go to Ad Council president and CEO Peggy Conlon for signing our 'Great Ape Humane Pledge,' committing never to use great apes in ads," Sean Conner wrote. "PETA will be following up with the CEOs of all the top U.S. ad agencies that sit on the Ad Council's executive board, requesting that they follow suit."

Later that month, *The New York Times* published a piece about a PETA investigation. "In what is becoming an annual Thanksgiving rite, an animal rights group on Tuesday released undercover videotapes taken at the nation's premier poultry-breeding operation, showing turkeys being stomped to death and punched by workers," McNeil Jr. wrote. According to the chronology on PETA's website, this led to "the first felony charges for abusing factory-farmed poultry in U.S. history," and "the first factory farmers to be convicted of abusing turkeys."

Near the end of November, *The Burlington Times-News* ran an Associated Press story, which included PETA's request to President George W. Bush that traditionally 'pardoned' turkeys be sent to a sanctuary, instead of Disneyland. "You might be a lame duck," Ingrid was quoted as having written to Bush, "but you still have the power to help lame turkeys."

Ingrid called for solidarity in an email to a sympathetic columnist, according to a December piece printed by *The Santa Fe New Mexican*. "Those of us who work for animals at any level are bound by a common bond," she wrote. "We must stick together against those who try to create rifts, often people who are professional animal exploiters who fear that we are a mighty force if united!" It's unclear to what exactly Ingrid was responding, but the columnist had apparently asked about PETA's stance on putting healthy animals to death in an earlier interview.

Later that month, *The Globe and Mail* ran a profile of Ingrid, in which she provided a rare glimpse of her nonprofessional life. For instance, PETA's co-founder recalled consulting with a loved one prior to making her unique will. "I got my mother's permission," Ingrid said. "She is a very practical person." The animal-rights crusader seemed to reference Neal Barnard, without naming him. "I have been in a steady relationship for 24 years," she said—before making a joke, noting her romantic partner wasn't a chimpanzee. "They are far too aggressive and hairy."

Also in December, Kalista Barter started working for PETA. During her time with the organization, she participated in the type of scantily-clad protest which some critics saw as degrading. "I certainly sat in a bloody tank outside of a McDonalds in a bikini," Kalista told this writer. "I saw that it worked. It got attention. It got the issue of animal rights on people's TV screens during the evening news." She didn't find the experience demeaning. "This is something that I believe brings awareness," Kalista said. "If I can lend my body to that cause, I'm very happy to do it."

PETA successfully petitioned an upscale restaurant to release a lobster estimated to be 140 years old, according to an Associated Press article, printed by *The Tribune-Democrat* in January of 2009. "We applaud the folks at City Crab and Seafood for their compassionate decision to allow this noble old-timer to live out his days in freedom and peace," Ingrid said. The unsigned article stated the creature would be released where lobster hunting wasn't allowed.

Later that month, *The Winnipeg Free Press* published an Associated Press brief, reporting PETA canceled its plan to shoot an anti-dogfighting advertisement with Vick, following his release from prison. The athlete's lawyers had insisted PETA support Vick's return to the National Football League. "Saying sorry and getting his ball back after being caught enjoying killing dogs in hideously cruel ways for many years doesn't cut it," Ingrid said. "Commissioner Goodell knows that he has an obligation to the league and to millions of fans, including children who look up to ballplayers as idols, to make sure that Michael Vick is mentally capable of remorse before he can touch, let alone wear, an NFL uniform again."

The Bolivian minister of defense announced a ban on the abuse of animals in military training exercises, according to an April blog post on PETA's website. "This news comes as a direct result of PETA's and PETA Germany's campaigns, which were launched after horrific video footage was uncovered showing the Bolivian military's mutilation and killing of dogs in combat-training exercises," Shawna Flavell wrote. "More than 20,000 supporters joined in the effort, including a leading Bolivian congresswoman, Ximena Flores Castro, who talked with PETA and then met with the defense minister to get the resolution on the books."

In July, *The New York Times* printed an article, in which Ingrid appeared unsure of how to respond to Vick's approaching reinstatement by the NFL. She wouldn't provide a definitive answer as to whether PETA would picket the athlete's games. "We may, I can't really say," Ingrid told Rhoden. "There are so many strong sentiments. It's on the table, but we're not encouraging it." However, she did reassert her prior recommendations. "We continue to ask Mr. Goodell to put [Vick] through psychological counseling and testing to see if he can be remorseful," Ingrid said. "We still want cruelty to animals to be part of the personal conduct policy for the NFL."

According to a September blog post published on PETA's website, the European Chemicals Agency instituted new standards that would prevent a massive loss of life. "The agency that oversees the largest animal testing program of all time has just announced new guidelines that mean that the number of animals who could fall victim to toxicity testing during the program has dropped—by 4.5 million," Flavell wrote. "This news from the European Chemicals Agency (ECHA) comes in response to a detailed letter PETA initiated in cooperation with other animal protection groups." The letter demonstrated many required tests were redundant.

PETA named Baltimore the 'Most Progressive Public School District of 2009,' according to an October brief in *The Baltimore Sun*. This was in response to the city's decision to serve vegetarian meals once a week, because of health, financial and environmental considerations. Animal-welfare didn't seem to play a role in the choice. Nevertheless, Ingrid praised the district's food and nutrition director. "By adopting 'Meatless Mondays,' Mr. Geraci is helping students develop healthy eating habits and saving animals' lives at the same time," she said. "Baltimore should be proud that its schools are considering how our food choices affect us—as well as the world around us."

Later that month, *The Winnipeg Free Press* ran a column by Ingrid, describing the disconnect otherwise-compassionate people had toward animals. "A few winters ago, I spoke at an international conference on non-violence," PETA's co-founder recounted. "Dinner was lamb. The mouths of people who spoke of ending violence were full of the bodies of animals whose throats had been slit with a knife." She continued, pointing out it was up to compassionate people to advance the nonhuman cause. "The animals cannot rise up to claim consideration," Ingrid wrote. "They have no power to bring about a revolution. They can only bleat and squeal when they are attacked."

In November, *The Hindustan Times* covered PETA's support for change made by an Indian institution. "By banning the use of elephants in zoos and circuses, the Central Zoo Authority has established itself as a world leader in elephant protection and has gone a long way towards ensuring that this magnificent animal will be allowed to lead a more natural and peaceful life," Ingrid said. "The Central Zoo Authority should be proud of the example that it has set for governments around the world. We are proud to honor the organization with PETA's Proggy Award for International Leadership, and we commend it for its initiative and kindness."

The Anderson Herald Bulletin printed an Associated Press report in December, regarding the seizure of 26,000 creatures from an exotic animal dealer. The dealer's attorneys claimed an undercover PETA agent, who exposed the abuse, neglected the animals to advance his investigation. Ingrid dismissed this, saying the dealer was attempting "to pin the blame for a litany of horrors on the one person who actually cared about the animals." According to the chronology on PETA's website, this was the largest seizure of animals in history.

14

THE HOLLYWOOD SCENE

In January of 2010, *The Washington Examiner* reported PETA accused the Washington Humane Society of ignoring calls regarding unwanted animals, allowing disease outbreaks to become routine, and putting nonhumans to death in a painful manner. PETA's co-founder seemed wary of fallout from the allegations. "The worst thing that people can do is to be upset with the Washington Humane Society and stop taking animals to the shelter," she told journalist Michael Neibauer. "This is the time for the District to put its foot down and say, 'Give us service.' All this is is 'please do your job, do it diligently and do it humanely.'"

The Tarboro Daily Southerner published an Associated Press article later that month, covering PETA's decision to cancel an anti-fur campaign using First Lady Michelle Obama's image without her permission. Meanwhile, PETA called on the White House to oppose Ringling Bros. circus naming an elephant Baby Barack. "[He] is not even a year old," Ingrid was quoted as having written to the president. "But his curious and energetic childhood has been cut tragically short while Ringling attempts to profit from your popularity by putting him on the road to perform in the circus."

Still in January, Gary Francione posted a blog entry on his website, that was representative of his critique of PETA's gradualist approach. "Because animals are chattel property and have no inherent value, the only welfare reforms that are accepted are those that provide an economic benefit for us," he wrote. "PETA acknowledges this explicitly in its campaign for gassing poultry—that method of slaughter is much better economically for producers. So PETA has, in effect, become a partner with industry to make animal exploitation more efficient."

Near the end of that month, *The Saint John Telegraph-Journal* ran a story about a Canadian politician who floated the idea of prosecuting PETA for serious crimes. "A Liberal MP thinks the federal government should investigate a U.S.-based animal rights group under Canada's anti-terrorism laws after a pie was pushed into the face of Fisheries Minister Gail Shea," reporter John Lewandowski wrote. Ingrid didn't seem phased. "Mr. Byrne's reaction is a silly, chest-beating exercise," she wrote in an email to Lewandowski. "It is unlikely to impress anyone who has a heart for animals or who is bright enough to spot the difference between a bomb and a tofu cream pie."

Ingrid continued to push her strategy—of seeking nonhuman rights in the long term and animal-welfare improvements in the short term—to questionable lengths. For instance, she hailed slaughterhouse-designer Temple Grandin in a February column posted by The McClatchy-Tribune News Service. "Today she is one of the best-known advocates for autism education," Ingrid wrote. "I applaud Dr. Grandin for another reason, one that has angered some people who work in animal protection: I admire her work in the field of humane animal slaughter."

Bob Barker donated $2.5 million to PETA, allowing the organization to open a new office in Los Angeles, according to a March brief in *The Chicago Daily Herald*. "The retired game show host and spay and neuter champion will cut the ribbon Wednesday at the Bob Barker Building on Sunset Boulevard and Alvarado Street," the unsigned brief stated. "PETA President Ingrid E. Newkirk says Barker could have just given the group a refrigerator but instead he paid for an entire building to be renovated. The building will be home to the group's media, marketing, youth outreach, and campaign departments."

Later that month, the animal group posted a blog entry, celebrating a beverage maker's decision to stop testing on animals. "After more than two years of behind-the-scenes discussions with PETA, Japan's ITO EN, Ltd., the world's largest manufacturer of green tea—with more than $3 billion in annual sales and ranked by Deloitte among the top 250 global consumer-product companies—has recently gotten out of the animal-testing business," Karin Bennett wrote. According to the chronology on PETA's website, Lipton Tea stopped animal testing shortly after, following conversations with Ingrid's organization.

Near the end of March, PETA published a blog post, discussing the amendment of a Utah pound-seizure law. "This means that animal shelters are no longer required to turn over animals for use in cruel experiments," Flavell wrote. "These positive changes come on the heels of a recent PETA undercover investigation inside laboratories at the University of Utah. The shocking investigation revealed that each year, more than 100 homeless cats and dogs from govern-ment-run animal shelters in Utah are sold to the university for use in invasive, painful, and deadly experiments."

Restating a point she'd made previously, Ingrid argued there was no such thing as a meat-eating environmentalist, in a *Colorado Daily* column that ran in April. "Raising and killing animals for food wastes so many resources and causes so much destruction, it's hard to know where to begin," she wrote. "A 2006 United Nations report revealed that the livestock sector generates more green-house gasses than all the cars, trucks, trains, planes, and ships in the world combined. The report attributed 18 percent of annual worldwide greenhouse-gas emissions to farmed animals, but new research indicates that the figure actually could be much higher."

In June, The McClatchy-Tribune News Service posted a column, in which Ingrid offered another way to understand the BP oil spill. "BP has more than the loss of human life, livelihoods, and tourism to answer for," she wrote. "If the criminal investigation of BP and those who signed off on the drill-site inspection sheets and safety assurances shows willful fraud and deception, dereliction of duty, bribes or who knows what else, there is one additional set of crimi-nal charges that should be added to the list: cruelty to animals. For this is the largest case of cruelty to animals in U.S. history."

Ingrid mourned the death of West Virginia's senator in a July letter printed by *The Bluefield Daily Telegraph*. "With the passing of Sen. Robert Byrd, animals and the people who care about them have lost a long-standing and true friend," she wrote. "Byrd's soft spot for animals—which was fueled by his love for his little dog, Billy—was as legendary as the passionate speeches that he often made on their behalf. No one who saw the speech that he gave in response to the Michael Vick scandal can forget the way in which Byrd rightly condemned dogfighting."

Later that month, *The Don Mills National Post* reported the Montreal Film and TV Commission had denied a permit to PETA. "[A] municipal agency has blocked the planned launch of an animal-rights ad featuring a scantily clad Pamela Anderson because it is sexist," journalist Graeme Hamilton wrote. "A fervent supporter of People for the Ethical Treatment of Animals, she had planned to appear in an Old Montreal plaza today to unveil a poster showing her wearing a bikini with her body parts labeled as if they were cuts of meat."

Ingrid was quoted in the *National Post* article, taking issue with the decision. "Your body is something you should be able to use for anything that's not harmful to anyone else," she said. "This is not harmful to anyone else. It's in fact intended to stop harm to what Pam calls 'sisters under the skin', which are the most exploited animals in the meat business—the females."

In August, *The Winnipeg Free Press* ran a column by Ingrid, opposing a National Institutes of Health plan to bring research chimpanzees out of retirement and subject them to further tests. "Some of the animals are 60 years old," PETA's co-founder wrote. "Some are left over from the space program. Petitions and pleas by everyone from physicians, veterinarians, and primatologists to actors such as Gene Hackman have been ignored." She called on President Barack Obama to intervene on the animals' behalf.

Ingrid demanded freedom for Tilikum, a long-suffering orca at SeaWorld, in a September column for *The Ashtabula Star Beacon*. "He killed a human being—for the third time—earlier this year," the animal activist wrote. "Tilikum didn't give his keeper, Dawn Brancheau, a little playful toss or misjudge and hold her under water just a second too long for her to survive. He shook her like a rag doll, slammed her into the side of the pool, stopped her from surfacing and tore her body apart." Ingrid believed Tilikum knew what he was doing, and this attack was an expression of his anger at being held captive.

A few days later, *The New York Times* printed an Associated Press report, which covered the aftermath of a PETA investigation. "A North Carolina laboratory has stopped doing research and is surrendering all of its animals a week after an undercover video showed what activists allege were workers cruelly treating dogs, cats, and rabbits, federal regulators said," according to the unsigned report. "Dave Sacks, a United States Department of Agriculture spokesman, said officials were trying to find new homes for more than 200 animals that were at Professional Laboratory and Research Services Inc. He said it was the company's decision to stop research. The agency has started a formal investigation."

A couple of days after that, *The Orange County Register* published a brief, explaining how Ingrid had written a letter to Vice President Joe Biden after he delivered hot dogs to troops. "The next time you decide to honor our men and women in uniform, please give them veggie dogs or other nutritious, cholesterol-free vegan foods and leave fatty, artery-clogging meat off the menu," she said. "Approximately 27 percent of people between the ages of 17 and 24 are too fat for military service."

Still in September, *The Santa Fe New Mexican* ran an article, which seems to have originally appeared *in The Chicago Tribune*, reporting on FBI surveillance of PETA during President George W. Bush's administration. "The FBI's ham-handed attempt to catch us with our pants down ended up backfiring," Ingrid said, responding to the news. "As a result, the FBI was caught with its pants down." The government monitored other activist groups as well—such as Greenpeace, Catholic Worker, and the Thomas Merton Center in Pittsburgh.

Ingrid spoke about the importance of celebrity activism, in an Associated Press report, printed by *The Aiken Standard* later that month. "We're a totally celebrity-besotted society," Ingrid said. "Even if you don't want to look, you have to see what they're up to . . . They're enormously powerful, and for them to have a compassionate voice for animals is a godsend." (Attempts to interview for this book some of PETA's most-famous, longtime celebrity supporters—like Alec Baldwin and Pamela Anderson—were unsuccessful.)

In a conversation with this writer, Dan Mathews made clear Ingrid disliked the demands associated with wooing celebrities. "She hates it," he said. "That's why she always pushes me to do that. She is not a party person . . . She does not enjoy the Hollywood scene. She does not enjoy the entertainment business. She follows it as minimally as possible. But she's thrilled that others at the organization, such as myself, can handle that crowd a little bit more easily."

The animal group gained access to documents about proposed NASA research, according to an October article in the journal *Nature*. "The experiment would expose [squirrel monkeys] to charged-particle radiation to reproduce the effects of cosmic rays on astronauts during a mission to Mars and to understand the effects of such radiation on the primate central nervous system," reporter Adam Mann wrote. "But PETA and other animal-rights groups criticize the methodology of the proposed test." The chronology on PETA's website asserted this $1.75 million experiment was canceled in the wake of activist pressure.

Later that month, Melanie Joy—author of the influential book *Why We Love Dogs, Eat Pigs, and Wear Cows*—met Ingrid at a yoga conference. She recounted the meeting in an interview with this writer. "I didn't even really know what she looked like," Melanie said, noting they were in a van carrying conference speakers to the airport. "There was a dog who was stuck in the middle of the highway." Ingrid insisted the driver stop the car, so she could help the animal. Melanie, not recognizing PETA's co-founder, offered to go along with her. But Ingrid said she could handle the situation on her own.

A couple of days later, Melanie received an email from Ingrid. "It said, thank you for being the only person in the van who offered to come help me with the dog," Melanie told this writer. "I had no idea it was her. I was surprised that she even knew that I was me. I just remembered this woman who was so impassioned, and cared so much about this dog on the side of the road, that she was willing to potentially miss her flight." According to Melanie, Ingrid was unable to locate the dog.

Ingrid's organization resolved a conflict with a British tabloid, according to a press release archived on PETA UK's website. "After being challenged by PETA's legal team over a completely fabricated story alleging that PETA intended to pour animal blood on Victoria Beckham (aka Posh Spice) because she uses exotic skins in her line of handbags, London newspaper the *Daily Mirror* has retracted the story, apologized to PETA, and agreed to pay damages and cover the group's attorneys' fees," the release stated.

Ingrid was quoted in the same release. "Victoria doesn't need to be doused with 'blood'—she needs to spend five minutes watching PETA's exposé showing alligators being beaten to death with baseball bats and snakes being skinned while they're still conscious," she said. "No kind person can watch animals struggle and fight for their lives like these animals do and still support such cruelty. We're sure that Ms. Beckham simply hasn't seen the footage we sent her."

In December, *The Melbourne Age* published a letter from Ingrid, pointing out the connection between a recent human tragedy and animal exploitation. "Ocean biologists now believe that the sharks who attacked bathers at the Egyptian resort of Sharm el-Sheikh this week may have been drawn to the area to feed on sheep carcasses tossed overboard from a vessel carrying Australian sheep for sacrifice during Eid," she wrote. "The bodies of sheep that died during the grueling open sea journey started washing ashore last week. It is time to stop this vile transport of sheep from Australian shores for umpteen reasons, now including one dead and three injured human beings."

Ingrid discouraged donating to charities that gave animals to poor families abroad, in a column printed later that month by *Colorado Daily*. "With the holidays upon us, kind folks are opening their checkbooks in the spirit of helping others," PETA's co-founder wrote. "People who would like to help the hungry might consider supporting organizations such as Food First, The Fruit Tree Planting Foundation and The Hunger Project, which do not send animals into a life of misery but do work to change the policies that allow hunger and poverty to thrive."

In February of 2011, *The Charleston Post and Courier* reported a laboratory researching in-vitro meat had been closed after the lead scientist was accused of insubordination by the Medical University of South Carolina. Ingrid praised Dr. Vladimir Mironov's work while criticizing the school for not providing more information about the charge. "It's clear there's a huge ruckus going on there, but a lot of lives depend on this research," she told journalist Renee Dudley.

"They may not be on two legs, but they depend on Mironov being back at his lab bench."

PETA subsidized work in the laboratory, according to the same article in *The Charleston Post and Courier*. "Mironov's meat lab has attracted national and international exposure in the past month, following the arrival of a new researcher whose work is being funded by the animal rights group People for the Ethical Treatment of Animals," Dudley wrote. "PETA gave a three-year grant to Nicholas Genovese to make so-called 'cultured meat' available to the public, reducing the number of animals killed for human consumption."

This support demonstrated Ingrid's commitment to in-vitro meat technology—which had the potential to save more lives than protests, publicity stunts or undercover investigations ever could. Nicholas would go on to become a co-founder of Memphis Meats, a company on the forefront of efforts to mass produce flesh without slaughter. (Attempts to interview him for this book were unsuccessful.)

On the same day in February, *The Washington Post* published an article, describing how a letter from PETA seemed to result in quick action. "The Transportation Security Administration is canceling plans to recruit new workers at this year's Iditarod dog race in Alaska after complaints from animal rights activists prompted a media inquiry," journalist Ed O'Keefe wrote. "TSA had planned to recruit potential job seekers in the hope of filling airport-screener vacancies at 22 Alaskan airports, according to [Kristin Lee, a TSA spokeswoman]." Per usual, Ingrid was ready with a joke. "We are howling with delight," she said. "There are so many ways to create jobs, and exploiting dogs is not one of them."

After Osama bin Laden was killed, PETA posted a blog entry about candy featuring the Al-Qaeda leader's face. "When we sent these delicious dairy-free chocolates to troops on Afghanistan a couple of years ago, they were great for cravings and target practice," Michelle Sherrow wrote in May. "Now we're sending them to the Navy SEALs who took the terrorist down to show our appreciation."

Ronnie Lee saw this as an example of PETA's willingness to exploit jingoism. "I said, will PETA's tongues be brown from eating a chocolate bar or from licking the asses of the U.S. military?" he told this writer. "It had that attitude—like, U-S-A, U-S-A, that kind of thing—that I absolutely hate. It's kind of populist. They sometimes take a populist political position which isn't an ethical position."

In June, *The Beckley Register-Herald* ran a piece from Scripps Howard News Service, regarding an advertisement that PETA was trying to place on a billboard. It compared cooking animal flesh to a recent infanticide case, in which a woman microwaved her baby. Of course, Ingrid defended the idea. "We're horrified at the thought of microwaving a helpless baby and hope that this billboard will open hearts and minds to the grief of other mothers who have their babies torn away from them simply to satisfy humans' fleeting taste sensations," she was quoted as saying.

Kalista had recently become PETA's manager of donor relations. Speaking with this author, she suggested the organization's head-line-grabbing tactics could be controversial even among contributors. "Some would write—upset about why we had done something or other—and others would say great job," Kalista recalled.

In May, Bruce Friedrich, by then a PETA vice president, left the organization to work at Farm Sanctuary. Ingrid tried to change his mind. "She was disappointed—[and] made a couple of suggestions for ways that perhaps I could come to PETA and continue to stay—but overall very supportive," he told this writer. Bruce came to regret leaving, and his experience with Farm Sanctuary's larger board gave him a new appreciation for PETA's setup.

In July, *The St. Louis Post Dispatch* printed a story about Nicholas beginning work at the University of Missouri's Division of Animal Sciences, still utilizing the PETA grant. Ingrid pushed back against outrage from local animal-exploiters. "He's decided to hang his hat in your neck of the woods," she told reporter Georgina Gustin, "and this has put the wind up the skirts of these farmers who are getting all panicky and apparently haven't been following trends in eating."

Ingrid—accurately or not—suggested there was a near consensus in support of Nicholas' research. "This is the wave of the future," she was quoted as saying in the same *St. Louis Post-Dispatch* story. "People who are environmentally aware are keen on this, animal rights advocates are keen on this, health advocates are keen on this. The only people who aren't keen are in a business that this will affect."

Ingrid reiterated her preference that feral cats be to death, rather than participate in trap-neuter-return programs, according to an article published later that month by *The New York Times*. "We call it T.N.A., which is trap, neuter and abandon," she told journalist Sydney Ember. "Wishful thinking isn't doing the job."

In an undated post to his website, no-kill leader Nathan Winograd compared Ingrid to nurses who kill their patients: "Were Newkirk to independently seek out thousands of animals a year by lying to people, answering free to good home ads, taking them from rescue groups and shelters, gathering animals through trapping, or acquiring those displaced by natural disasters, only to inject them with poison and kill them—it would be immediately obvious to everyone that she was a deeply disturbed woman." (Attempts to interview Nathan for this book were unsuccessful.)

In August, *The New York Times* reported on the treatment of an anti-speciesist prisoner. "Dave McDonald 70, of Mill Valley, has been a vegetarian for 42 years. But when he was jailed recently for 99 days on drug-related charges (most of which were later dropped), Mr. McDonald was denied vegetarian meals," journalist James Scott wrote. "He refused to eat anything that he did not know was animal-free, and as a result, his weight plummeted nearly 50 pounds to 155." Referring to this as cruel and unusual punishment, Ingrid seemed to threaten the county with a lawsuit. "We would certainly be willing to help him," she said. "A moral position is as strong as a religious conviction."

Ingrid recounted the aftermath of a natural disaster, in a September column distributed by McClatchy-Tribune News Service. "In the course of a few days recently, PETA's headquarters in Norfolk, Virginia, was rocked by a 5.8-magnitude earthquake and then clobbered by Hurricane Irene," she wrote. "Half of the underside of our headquarters blew away and renting out rafts on the river that was once our road could have kept us in dog treats for a year. Luckily, all the building's occupants, including Brandi, Bubbles and Marshall, the cats who live on the top floor, emerged unscathed." Ingrid went on to describe her organization's rescue efforts.

Later that month, PETA posted a blog entry on its website, about an undercover investigation it had conducted at a ferret-breeding facility. "PETA found that Triple F's owners, supervisors, and workers left ferrets with bleeding rectal prolapses, gaping wounds, herniated organs, painful mammary gland infections, and ruptured, bleeding eyes to suffer and die without veterinary care," Lindsay Pollard-Post stated. The chronology on PETA's website asserted this investigation resulted in more than $44,000 worth of federal fines and payments for Triple F Farms.

Still in September, *The Orange County Register* highlighted a letter Ingrid wrote to the Duchess of Cambridge, asking her to stop Prince William from giving 250 animals to his brother for a shooting party. "There is no honor in buying birds and reducing them, as if they were clay pigeons, to shooting targets," Ingrid said in her message. "Those who aren't killed outright are often dispatched by having their necks wrung, which does not cause an instant or painless death."

The military stopped using nonhumans for nerve-agent training, according to an October post on PETA's blog. "Instead of abusing terrified monkeys, Aberdeen—the only Army base in the country that uses animals for this training—will now use human patient simulators, just as every other military facility already does," Heather Faraid Drennan wrote. "The move follows months of vigorous campaigning by PETA."

In October, *The Orlando Sentinel* published an article about PETA's plan to sue SeaWorld. "The animal-rights group PETA is expected to file a federal lawsuit in California this week alleging that SeaWorld Parks & Entertainment is violating the U.S. Constitution's ban on slavery by keeping five wild-caught killer whales at marine parks in Orlando and San Diego," journalist Jason Garcia wrote. Ingrid argued legal changes made in the aftermath of the American Civil War should apply to animals. "The 13th Amendment prohibits slavery, and these orcas are, by definition, slaves," she said.

The founder of the Nonhuman Rights Project, Steven Wise, referred to the 13th-Amendment lawsuit as a setback, in a November blog post on his organization's website. "There are three major problems with filing such suits as 'a show,'" he wrote. "First, they create unfavorable law where no law previously existed and erect an obstacle that lawyers who are not putting on a show, but who are litigating to win, will be later forced to overcome. Second, the public, including perhaps some judges, may confuse 'a show' with the real McCoy. Third, the PETA suit was sloppily drafted, twice confusing common law with the Supreme Court's interpretation of the 13th Amendment."

In November, FoxNews.com ran an Associated Press story, regarding a $270,000 fine that the owner of Ringling Bros. circus agreed to pay. "The U.S. Department of Agriculture says the civil penalty announced Monday is the largest ever assessed against an animal exhibitor under the Animal Welfare Act," the unsigned piece stated. "People for the Ethical Treatment of Animals, which has filed numerous complaints with USDA against the circus, especially for its handling of elephants, said the fine is a good first step. But it called on the government to confiscate the elephants." In the organizational chronology posted to its website, PETA took credit for the record-setting fine, claiming it provided the necessary evidence to the government.

That same month, *The Christian Science Monitor* reported Ingrid endorsed lifting a ban on horse slaughter—a counterintuitive position that seemed to prematurely concede outlawing the export of horses for meat was impossible. "As Newkirk predicted, the end to domestic slaughter didn't curtail the number of horses being slaughtered for consumption, but, according to a GAO report, may have led to more inhumane treatment of old, abandoned, or neglected equines as greater numbers were instead shipped to Mexico or Canada for slaughter where the USDA doesn't have the authority to monitor the horses' conditions," journalist Patrik Jonsson wrote.

According to a Canadian Press article, printed in December by *The Winnipeg Free Press*, Ingrid slammed presidential candidate Mitt Romney for putting his dog in a crate, which he secured to the roof of his station wagon for a 12-hour drive. "If you wouldn't strap your child to the roof of your car, you have no business doing that to the family dog," she said. "I don't know who would find that acceptable." However, she apparently grew tired of talking about the incident, requesting people focus on core issues facing animals when asked about it later.

Before the end of the year, *The Washington Post* ran a story about Walter Rave, an early PETA activist who succumbed to injuries suffered while trying to rescue his cats from a fire. Ingrid called him in the hospital twice. "I said, 'Walt, you're deeply loved and you're a kind soul that no one will ever forget," she recounted, noting the activist designed PETA's first T-shirt. "He drew two—a bunny sitting on a hill and an animal's paw next to the Black Power fist. We went with the bunny."

15

EVEN COWS WITH NAMES

In January of 2012, *The McCallen Monitor* published a column by Ingrid, presumably timed to celebrate Martin Luther King Jr. Day. "When King protested the Vietnam War, black clergy admonished him and said that he should stay out of it, that it was a different issue," PETA's co-founder wrote, adding the civil-rights icon saw various forms of domination as interconnected. "We must stop thinking of animal rights as less deserving of our energy than other struggles for social justice. All oppression, prejudice, violence, and cruelty are wrong, and when we witness it, we must never be silent."

Later that month, PETA posted a blog entry, with good news from a United States territory. "In the triumphant finale to a long, hard legal struggle over a suit filed by PETA and citizens of Guayama, Puerto Rico, the Puerto Rican Supreme Court upheld the decisions of the lower courts that the monkey-breeding facility built in Guayama by Bioculture, Inc., was constructed illegally and therefore cannot be opened for business," the unsigned entry stated. "The court also denied Bioculture's motion to reconsider the ruling."

In a March letter printed by *The Tallahassee Democrat*, Ingrid urged Governor Rick Scott to veto a bill that would allow people to dye animals. "If dying is approved, animals will suffer," PETA's co-founder wrote. "The novelty of a pink rabbit or green chick lasts only as long as a child's attention span. Senate Democratic Leader Nan Rich reasonably pointed out that dying animals should violate Florida's anti-cruelty statutes, and our office has been flooded with calls from Floridians who are aghast to learn of this pending debacle."

That same month, *The New York Times* discussed the cancellation of an HBO series, after a number of horses were killed during the production. "At advocacy groups like People for the Ethical Treatment of Animals, there is a Cassandra-like feeling that frequent warnings about conditions [on the show's set] were not heeded until it was too late," journalist Dave Itzkoff wrote. "Necropsy reports on these horses, prepared by the California Animal Health and Food Safety Laboratory System, raised further concerns with PETA." Ingrid's organization went public with information it learned from whistle-blowers, according to the chronology on PETA's website.

The Coast Guard defended its use of animals in medical training, The Associated Press reported in an April piece published by CBSNews.com. "PETA said the undercover video it released from a whistleblower did show military instructors contracted by the Coast Guard cutting off an anesthetized goat's legs in Virginia Beach," the unsigned piece stated. "PETA and other animal rights groups, as well as some medical professionals, say the practice is cruel and unnecessary. They promote the use of human simulation models over animals." PETA's chronology asserted the contractors were cited for violating the Animal Welfare Act.

In June, *The Washington Post* ran a story about a laboratory—formerly called SEMA—which Ingrid's group had tangled with in the past. "Just four chimps remain at this controversial research facility near Interstate 270 in Rockville," reporter Brian Vastag wrote. "The company's 30-year run of chimpanzee research is ending, the victim of a historic shift away from using apes in medical experiments." This came after PETA acquired $1,000 of the laboratory's stock, giving activists the right to attend shareholders' meetings.

Ingrid's organization announced some good news in a July press release, archived on the PETA UK website. "Following discussions with PETA US—and after receiving e-mails from thousands of its supporters—top cosmetics company Urban Decay has canceled previously announced plans to begin marketing its products in China, where cruel and deadly animal tests are currently required by the government," the release stated. "Urban Decay has been returned to the Humane Cosmetics Standard endorsed by PETA UK and will also receive PETA US' Courage in Commerce Award."

Ingrid praised the move. "Urban Decay is a corporate champion in PETA's book for refusing to pay for animals to be harmed and killed for the sake of overseas profits," she said in the same press release. "The company's ethical decision also reveals the moral decay of other larger companies that have sold animals out for a market share in China."

In the wake of a PETA lawsuit, the American government adopted new regulations, according to a blog entry, posted to the animal group's website later that month. "For decades, the U.S. Fish and Wildlife Service (FWS) illegally and quietly issued captive-bred wildlife permits—allowing circuses, roadside zoos, and others to harm, harass, and wound captive-bred endangered species and making it almost impossible to challenge these abuses," the unsigned post stated. "We asked the court to require the FWS to make those applications publicly available and to consider public comments before making a decision about whether to approve any application."

That same day, *The London Daily Mirror* published a letter from Ingrid, condemning research in which kittens' eyes were sewn shut. "Cardiff University will only draw international ridicule for this kind of cruel, archaic and failed approach," she wrote. "The fact the Home Office granted a license for the tests is a sign public opinion counts for nothing in regulating experiments. The secrecy clause in the law that keeps the public from finding out what kind of misery their taxes are funding must be removed."

Air China agreed to stop transporting research monkeys, according to an August media statement on PETA UK's website. "The supply of monkeys to animal laboratories is a global business, dependent on the handful of airlines still willing to dirty their hands with this trade," Ingrid said. "Now that Air China is no longer participating in this bloody trade, experimenters will find it harder to get their hands on more victims. PETA will continue to pressure airlines worldwide to follow Air China's lead and stop delivering primates to certain suffering and death."

Later that month, PETA posted a blog entry about its donation of medical-training equipment to an Egyptian facility, which would have otherwise killed goats during exercises. "While Dr. Elkholy wanted to switch to Simulab Corporation's TraumaMan simulator for [his Advanced Trauma Life Support course], budget limitations kept him from making the transition," the unsigned post stated. "PETA was pleased to donate three TraumaMan simulators—thanks to the generous support of the McGrath Family Foundation—so that the [Egyptian Life Support Training Center] can conduct ATLS courses without using any animals."

Ingrid accused a columnist of romanticizing organic dairy farms, in a letter *The New York Times* ran in September. "I applaud his recognition that cows are individual feeling beings that share with us the ability to experience happiness and contentment, fear and pain," she wrote. "The article does, however, gloss over the undeniable fact that even cows with names produce milk only because they have recently given birth to calves who, if male, have been taken away from them. Consumers should consider that cows like Edie or Sophia are often fiercely protective, grieving mothers whose anguished cries the farmer undoubtedly heard as he removed their young."

In October, *The Times of India* previewed Ingrid's upcoming protest against horse-drawn carriages. "Newkirk is flying to Mumbai from her Washington headquarters to tie herself to a Victoria chariot like a horse," reporter Vijay Singh wrote. "Horses used to pull carriages are frequently denied adequate rest, food, and water and are kept in filthy, damp stables infested with biting insects. Many never see a veterinarian in their entire lives."

PETA's co-founder was quoted in *The Times of India* preview, making clear she sought more than reform. "Horses, like people, are made of blood, flesh, and bone and suffer when they are whipped and made to haul heavy loads that their malnourished bodies can hardly bear," Ingrid said. "The only way to ensure that these gentle animals don't suffer and that the safety of residents and tourists isn't placed at risk is to ban horse-drawn carriages."

Ingrid discussed what might be termed human privilege, in a November column printed by *The Frederick News-Post*, after the Powerball jackpot rose to hundreds of millions of dollars. "Just imagine for one moment what life would be like if you had been born a mouse in a laboratory, a dog kept outside on a chain this winter, a bear in a barren enclosure in a roadside zoo or a bird confined to a cage," she wrote. "This is an appeal to all of us who have won life's lottery by being born into the luckiest 0.0001 percent of life forms: Remember to care and share, especially during this season of goodwill, Powerball or no Powerball."

Near the end of that month, *The Washington Examiner* ran a brief about Ingrid's criticism of Republican Congressman Paul Ryan, who had taken his ten-year-old daughter hunting. "You can't teach kids to be tough, if that was the purpose, by encouraging them to kill those who can't defend themselves," PETA's co-founder wrote to the former vice-presidential nominee. "I suspect that while you love your daughter, you don't understand that the love of one's offspring is shared by other living beings, including deer, whose fawns become orphaned when they are killed."

In December, *The Riverside Press-Enterprise* published an article, about a governmental raid on a company that bred reptiles and rodents. "On Thursday afternoon, officers were still at the property, which was blocked off with yellow caution tape," reporter Sarah Burge wrote. "The stench from the building filled the parking lot as workers in protective suits and masks came and went." The chronology on PETA's website asserted this action, which came as result of the group's investigation, led to "the largest rescue of neglected rats in U.S. history and the largest seizure of animals, including more than 600 reptiles and 18,000 rats, ever in California."

Later that month, *The Belfast Telegraph* printed a piece by Ingrid, in which she placed blame for nonhuman deaths during production of *The Hobbit: An Unexpected Journey* on the film's director. "[Peter] Jackson has even less of an excuse than most: he's the Gandalf of computer-generated imagery," PETA's co-founder wrote. "Yet he's playing the role of Sauron, wielding power and control over animals simply because he can. Technology has changed the direction of movie-making with astonishing speed and precision. Those who still resort to using live animals will be left behind faster than that kid in *Home Alone*."

Still in December, *The Washington Examiner* covered an upcoming protest. "People for the Ethical Treatment of Animals wants to take the gun control debate to a whole new level: banning hunting," journalist Paul Bedard wrote. "The group plans to make their case Friday by crashing the National Rifle Association's press conference downtown at the Willard Hotel." Ingrid condemned the gun-rights organization. "The NRA's culture of cruelty instills violence in society by promoting the shooting of animals for fun, and this must be stopped," she said. "It's time we face the fact that as we strive for a more peaceful world, we must tackle all forms of senseless killing—and that includes hunting."

The Winchester Star ran an Associated Press story in February of 2013, detailing PETA's plan to rename its Virginia headquarters after Sam Simon, co-creator of *The Simpsons*. Speaking with this writer, Kalista suggested Ingrid's decision wasn't tied to any specific donation. "She and Sam Simon had known each other for a long, long, long time," Kalista said. "He was dying. It was something she really wanted to do for him, while he was still alive, to honor all that he had done for PETA and for animals. That was a hard loss for her."

PETA intended to buy remote-controlled aircraft to monitor hunters, according to a *Hutchinson News* piece that ran in April. "The talk is usually about drones being used as killing machines, but PETA drones will be used to save lives," Ingrid said. "Slob hunters may need to rethink the idea that they can get away with murder, alone out there in the woods with no one watching." The animal group also planned to use the aircraft to surveil factory farms.

That summer, Kalista left PETA. "I think Ingrid slept five hours a night," she told this writer. "I'd be working until seven at night [in California] and she's still emailing me on the East Coast. I'd get up in the morning and have a whole bunch of emails from her already, starting at 5 a.m." Kalista couldn't keep up. "Working so closely with somebody that I respected so much—and seeing her level of commitment to the cause—made me feel like I've got to work as hard as her," she said. "That wasn't sustainable."

In July, *USA Today* posted an article on its website, regarding a federal investigation into a slaughterhouse. The probe followed PETA's release of footage taken inside the facility. "The two-minute clip shows a worker incorrectly stunning sows with an electrical wand and causing them apparent suffering in violation of federal law," journalist Emily Le Coz wrote. "The Humane Methods of Slaughter Act states four-legged animals must be quickly and painlessly stunned before they're slaughtered." According to PETA's chronology, the slaughterhouse was ultimately shut down.

Later that month, *Mother Jones* reported PETA was amongst a group of plaintiffs challenging a Utah law that effectively criminalized whistleblowing in the agriculture industry. "Proponents of the law have argued that this is a private property issue and that activists should not be allowed to record on someone's property without their consent," journalist Zaineb Mohammed wrote. "But the plaintiffs say the law is designed to prevent the exposure of abuse at agricultural facilities."

In August, *The Sitka Daily Sentinel* ran an Associated Press piece, about the first public taste testing of an in-vitro meat hamburger. "As long as there's anybody who's willing to kill a chicken, a cow or a pig to make their meal, we're all for this," Ingrid said. "Instead of the millions and billions (of animals) being slaughtered now, we could just clone a few cells to make burgers or chops." A little over a week later, *The Walla Walla Union-Bulletin* printed a column in which Ingrid predicted cultured flesh would be commercially viable in less than a decade.

That same month, Mary Ward died, according to a September obituary published by *The Eugene Register-Guard*. Ingrid's mother would have been approximately 92 years old. "Ward is predeceased by her husband, her beloved dogs Shauny, Gus, Flip and Peaches, and survived by her daughter," the remembrance stated. "In honor of her wishes, no service will be held. Donations to PETA in lieu of flowers would make her smile."

Also in September, *The Ashtabula Star Beacon* ran a column by Ingrid, dismissing public concern about shelters' save rates. "To reduce the number of animals it euthanizes, a shelter must reduce the number of animals it takes in by charging high 'surrender' fees, putting people on waiting lists, sending unsterilized animals to 'foster' homes and more," PETA's co-founder wrote. "To truly save dogs' and cats' lives, let's reject this shelter 'save-rate' nonsense and get to the root of the problem: the population explosion. Open-admission shelters, solid animal-control services, community education, and reduced-cost spay-and-neuter programs are the keys to a real 'save' rate."

The Harrisonburg Daily News-Record printed an Associated Press article in October, reporting that the FBI investigated PETA in the

1990s, fearing the animal group planned to release anthrax at the United States Army Medical Research Institute of Infectious Diseases. "I was bowled over by it," Ingrid said of the revelation. "It was such a disappointment. I don't know if someone just hated us, but it's *Alice in Wonderland*. It's total fantasy." The FBI apparently received a tip, claiming the animal group moved its headquarters from Maryland to Virginia to avoid exposure to the infection.

Ingrid was paraphrased in the October Associated Press article, describing the government's repressive—and at times head-scratching—interactions with PETA over the years. "Newkirk said that her international travel was tracked and PETA demonstrations were monitored," the unsigned article stated. "The group's headquarters were photographed and were under surveillance, and it was asked for the building's security codes. She said that the FBI once inquired about the thickness of the building's windows and whether they would withstand bullets."

In November, *The Times of India* ran a piece about Ingrid, who had recently given a lecture in Delhi. Speaking with reporter Aanchal Tuli, PETA's co-founder indulged in a bit of nostalgia. "I have come here after a really long time but I still feel at home," she said. "I don't recognize everything, but I can still make out the roads to Connaught Place and Ashoka Hotel. These pavements, where I used to ride my bike during my summer vacations, those paths, are still familiar to me."

In the same *Times of India* piece, Ingrid argued celebrity activism was important in that country. "Not just in Bollywood, but in Hollywood also, people want to see and know what a celeb is endorsing," she told Tuli. "It's what gets people to come back and research online, to see what that campaign is about and to extend support to us. In India, where Bollywood is like a religion, the celeb attachment to a campaign makes a lot of difference. So when Shilpa Shetty sits in a cage, or when John Abraham protests being caged, people do take interest."

PETA posted a blog entry in December, about a large clothing company's decision to stop carrying certain items. "After discussions with PETA, PVH Corp.—the parent company of Calvin Klein, Tommy Hilfiger, IZOD, ARROW, Van Heusen, and other brands—has confirmed that it's pulling from its shelves and banning any products made with angora," the unsigned article stated. "The announcement follows the release of video footage—shot by a PETA Asia investigator in China, the source of 90 percent of the world's angora fur—that shows workers violently ripping the fur from the bodies of screaming rabbits."

16

JEFFREY DAHMER'S HOME

In February of 2014, *The Ashtabula Star Beacon* published a column by Ingrid, attacking the Westminster Kennel Club dog show for contributing to the problem of pet overpopulation. "We have more than enough dogs to go around—far too many to place them all in loving homes or indeed in any homes," she wrote, noting breeders ultimately caused more animals to be killed in shelters. "But the pedigree dogs who compete in Westminster don't get much out of the deal, either. They are bred with [serious health] problems that become manifest later in life."

In March, *The Financial Times* ran a letter from Ingrid, pushing back on the notion in-vitro meat was fake. "It's real meat made from real pig, cow and—one day—chicken cells," she wrote. "But unlike meat that comes from animals which suffer miserable lives in disease-ridden pens and cages and end up on killing floors covered with feces, in-vitro meat is produced in the laboratory and so eliminates the risk of contamination with salmonella, E. coli, and the other pathogens that cause massive meat recalls when many people become ill or large numbers of fatalities occur."

Later in the month, *The London Express* reported a jockey had referred to horses as replaceable, infuriating Ingrid. "Walsh's comments expose the true emotion behind horse racing: greed," she said. "They are deeply offensive to anyone who has ever loved and lost a horse or other beloved animal companion. Horses are treated like wind-up toys, their fragile limbs pushed to and sometimes beyond the breaking point, and are overworked to the detriment of their health by the inherently cruel and greedy racing business, where money is king. Every year, hundreds of horses come a cropper and die on British racetracks, only to be casually discarded."

Still in March, *The Guelph Mercury* published a column by Ingrid, celebrating a labor leader who was the subject of a soon-to-be-released biopic. "Cesar Chavez is an American hero, and I had the honor of meeting him 30 years ago when PETA (People for the Ethical Treatment of Animals) presented him with an award for recognizing that nonviolence begins with what we eat," she wrote. "To really honor the Chavez legacy, we should follow in his footsteps and stop eating animals, his friends. Although he is best known as the founder of the United Farm Workers of America, Chavez's passion for justice did not stop with humans."

Ingrid asked about transforming serial killer Jeffrey Dahmer's home into a vegan restaurant, according to an April piece in *The Akron Beacon Journal*. "We are always looking for ways to draw attention to the violence inherent in the production of meat, eggs, and milk—which involve processes that would shock all but the most hard-hearted person," Newkirk was quoted as having written to a real-estate agent. "Dahmer's old house gives us a way to evoke sympathy for these victims and to suggest that a life-affirming diet can change everything."

The next day, *The London Daily Mirror* ran a letter from Ingrid, apparently responding to comments made by Princess Anne, who supported the use of poison gas in the badger cull and boosted the horse-meat trade as a means of improving nonhuman welfare. "Instead of devising ways to dispense with animals, the Princess should use her considerable influence to advocate changes that will improve their lives," PETA's co-founder wrote. "Those who have everything in life should not be calling for the deaths of horses and badgers, whose only crime is to be born into a world where humans are in charge." Ingrid's letter is somewhat perplexing, given she'd recently supported legalizing horse slaughter in the United States.

Still in April, *The Gaston Gazette* printed an article from McClatchy-Tribune Information Services, reporting the realtor who listed Dahmer's home had called Ingrid's bluff. "The real estate agent, Richard Lubinski of Stouffer Realty, said Tuesday that he was not surprised that PETA dropped the proposal," the unsigned article stated. "Lubinski noted that in 2012, PETA said that it wanted to turn the Florida home of O.J. Simpson into a 'Meat is Murder Museum.' The home was in foreclosure, and PETA asked the bank if it would donate or sell the home to the group. Simpson was acquitted in 1995 on murder charges in the killing of his ex-wife and her friend."

PETA released a video of Australian shearers abusing nonhumans, according to a July piece in *mX*. "These sheep were punched in the face, kicked and stamped on and had their heads slammed into the floor by unsupervised, impatient shearers, causing them great distress and injury," Ingrid said. "PETA is calling on shoppers around the world to reject cruelty to animals—and that means never buying wool." The footage seems to have been so awful that Australian Wool Innovation also condemned the abuse.

That same month, *The Northwest Florida Daily News* ran a story about a PETA stunt, in which a plane pulled a banner along the shore. Its message was: 'Keep hookers off the beach—No fishing!' This tongue-in-cheek text came in response to a shark biting someone who swam beside surf fishermen. "Fishing is a dangerous blood sport that threatens all coastal wildlife as well as residents and tourists visiting Florida beaches," Ingrid told reporter Tom McLaughlin.

Following the release of *Blackfish*, the landmark documentary about Tilikum, Southwest Airlines cut ties with SeaWorld, according to *an* Associated Press piece, published in August by *The Traverse City Record-Eagle*. Ingrid and her staff celebrated the decision. "Champagne corks were popping at PETA when we heard that Southwest will no longer support SeaWorld and will repaint its planes," she said. "The second I heard the good news, I knew that I'd be booking my next trip on Southwest."

Later that month, *The Elyria Chronicle-Telegram* printed a column by Ingrid, in which she responded to the controversy surrounding PETA's offer to pay the water bills of select Detroit residents if they went vegan for a month. "When news hit that Detroit was cutting off water to thousands of residents who were behind in paying their bills, the critics, not surprisingly came out in full force," Ingrid wrote, apparently feigning shock. "What might surprise you is that some of those throwing stones were aiming not at city officials but at PETA—after one of our members hit upon a way to help both struggling families and animals."

Still in August, *The London Daily Mail* ran a letter from Ingrid, defending her organization's proposed billboard, which was inspired by the discovery of human remains in an Irish recycling center. "How could one fail to recognize the parallel when bins across Dublin and the rest of the world are littered with the limbs of other unidentified individuals—all with feelings and formerly full of life— who were killed and dismembered for nothing more than a fleeting taste of flesh?" She wrote. "Isn't it a grand thing to want to extend our compassion to animals, to oppose violence in all its ugly forms?"

Ingrid planned to auction a family heirloom, according to a September article in *The Gloucestershire Echo*. "A 100-year-old bell, which once belonged to her great-uncle, will go up for sale on internet auction site eBay to raise cash for anti-cull campaigners," reporter David Shepherd wrote. "Ingrid's great-uncle Sidney was a former headmaster who would ring the bell from the steps of a grammar school in Coleford every morning."

Ingrid recalled how Sidney and her father loved the Forest of Dean, where the boar cull was scheduled to take place. "They knew its paths and peculiarities well and, as amateur ethologists and hobby botanists, appreciated the trees, plants, birds and other wildlife in it," she was quoted as saying, in the same *Gloucestershire Echo* article. "Both would be whirling in their graves at the thought that the wild boar were being cavalierly dismissed as 'pests' and would say that the real pests are the human interlopers who appreciate nothing natural, only artificial constructs and pleasures."

In October, PETA India posted a blog entry about the country's decision to ban the importation of cosmetics tested on nonhumans. "After intensive efforts by PETA India, Union Minister Maneka Gandhi and others, the Indian Ministry of Health & Family Welfare has made an announcement that will save millions of animals from being blinded, poisoned and killed," the unsigned entry stated. "The move brings India up to speed with Israel and the European Union nations, which have already banned the sale and marketing of animal-tested cosmetics. Earlier this year, the testing of cosmetics on animals was banned in India following efforts by PETA and others."

That same month, *The Straits Times* published an *Agence France-Presse* article, reporting on Taiwan's raid of a pigeon-racing club. "Agents from the Criminal Investigation Bureau last week searched the office of the club in the southern city of Kaohsiung and froze about NT$120 million (S$5.03 million) in assets," the unsigned article stated. "Police also detained three employees on charges of violating the animal protection law and illegal gambling. The move came in response to complaints from People for the Ethical Treatment of Animals (PETA) about the pigeon race gambling industry."

PETA proposed building a memorial to animals killed in an accident, according to piece printed by *The Orangeville Midweek Banner*, near the end of October. "About 400 turkeys died when a tractor-trailer carrying them tipped onto its side and crashed," the unsigned piece stated. "A letter on behalf of PETA and local animal rights group Toronto Pig Save has been sent to Erin roads superintendent Larry Van Wyck to request permission to erect a ten-foot-tall monument."

Ingrid was quoted in the same piece, explaining her group's rationale. "This memorial is intended to make roads safer for everyone by reminding tractor-trailer drivers of their responsibility to the thousands of animals they haul," she said. "PETA's motto reads, in part, that 'animals are not ours to eat,' and we're asking motorists to consider preventing other roadside tragedies by choosing healthy, delicious vegan foods."

In November, *The Times of India* covered a bit of street theater. "People for the Ethical Treatment of Animals (PETA) India founder, Ingrid Newkirk, willfully caged herself in Bandra on Thursday outside the American chicken-meat restaurant chain KFC to bring a powerful message to Mumbai at the start of World Vegan Month— that chickens killed for food endure immense stress and deprivation in filthy, cramped cages or sheds long before they're shipped to a slaughterhouse, where they die painfully," reporter Vijay Singh wrote.

Later that month, *The Times of India* published a follow-up, about a ten-year-old boy who had been inspired by Ingrid's protest. "He refused to allow his parents to kill and cook two chickens," Singh wrote. "Animal rights campaigners were surprised to see the boy, identified only as Johnny, bring the two birds to their office." Of course, Ingrid was pleased. "I am so glad that my demonstration in Bandra to promote healthy vegan food and highlight the plight of caged chickens has positively influenced the boy," she said. "We can't thank him enough and his parents."

In December, *The Winnipeg Free Press* ran a Canadian Press story, regarding PETA's attempt to place a provocative advertisement. "Earlier this week, a devoutly religious Hamilton woman pleaded guilty to failing to notify authorities that her husband had died from an illness for which he was not getting treatment," The Canadian Press reported, noting she kept her husband's body for six months, praying for his resurrection. PETA's proposed billboard read: 'Are There Corpses in Your Home? Time to Go Vegan.' Ingrid defended the promotion. "If you have chicken breasts, steaks or bologna in your refrigerator, we have news for you: you're sharing your home with corpses," she said.

According to a *Syracuse Post-Standard* brief, printed later that month, Ingrid demanded a college football player be punished. The athlete killed a raccoon after he tried to take a photo of himself with the animal and was bitten. "It's time for acts of cruelty to animals committed by players to be taken seriously, and with violence in football culture now under the microscope, this is the time to address the issue," Ingrid was quoted as having written. Her mention of violence in football culture appeared to reference the trial of a former New England Patriots tight end for murder.

Still in December, the co-founder of Direct Action Everywhere criticized PETA's dog-leather exposé on his organization's blog. "The campaign plays on racism to draw support, and undermines our attempts to inspire Chinese activists to take action," Wayne Hsiung wrote. "The PETA video, like so many other campaigns against Chinese practices, relies on an American-sounding narrator describing horrible abuses by the Chinese. It has the feel of a nature documentary, with dirty, violent, animalistic Asians contrasted with the calm, compassionate, English-speaking narrator."

Wayne continued, arguing the exposé was also speciesist. "It privileges dogs over other animals, and thereby reinforces the notion that human beings can arbitrarily decide which animals matter," he wrote in the same blog post. "Many say that focusing on industries such as dog leather, marginal though they may be, is strategic because it is the 'low hanging fruit'—easy to garner opposition to, and just as easy to destroy. This confuses the basic function of the activist. We are not here to be popular. We are not here to cater to existing views. We are here to challenge and change those views." (Attempts to interview Wayne for this book were unsuccessful.)

Tony Benn, a well-known socialist, was posthumously honored, according to a piece that appeared in *The Derbyshire Times*, near the end of the year. "The Labour politician, who died in March aged 88, has been named Peta UK's person of the year 2014," the unsigned piece stated. "During his 47 years in office, Mr. Benn, a vegetarian, came to the defense of animals on many occasions—voting against fox hunting in Parliament and protesting against experiments on animals in laboratories." Ingrid praised the leftist. "An outspoken defender of justice, his advocacy for animals helped open eyes, hearts, and minds," she said. "Mr. Benn has left a lasting legacy of respect for animals, for which we are deeply grateful."

In January of 2015, *The Farmington Daily Times* ran an Associated Press story, about a photograph that former vice-presidential nominee Sarah Palin posted online, featuring her 6-year-old child with Down syndrome standing on the family's dog. Ingrid was quoted, discussing the matter. "PETA simply believes that people shouldn't step on dogs, and judging by the reaction that we've seen to Sarah Palin's Instagram photo, we're far from alone in that belief," the animal group's co-founder said.

After a judge struck down California's ban on foie gras, Ingrid seemed to focus her ire at restaurateurs, according to a Tribune News Service article, published by *The Gaston Gazette* later that month. "Foie gras is French for 'fatty liver,' and 'fathead' is the American word for the shameless chefs who actually need a law to make them stop serving the swollen, near-bursting organ of a cruelly force-fed bird," she said. "A line will be drawn in the sand outside any restaurant that goes back to serving this 'torture in a tin' And whoever crosses that line identifies themselves with gluttony that cannot control itself even to the point of torturing animals."

Near the end of January, PETA posted a blog entry, announcing a successful end to an anti-vivisection campaign. "Following an intensive PETA campaign to expose and end cruel and archaic sound-localization experiments on cats at the University of

Wisconsin-Madison (UW), the federal grant money has expired, the lead experimenter has retired, and the embattled laboratory has closed its doors for good," Alisa Mullins wrote. "The remaining four cats in the laboratory, including three-year-old tabbies Rainbow and Mango, have been adopted into private homes."

Bowing to pressure from Ingrid's organization, a large retailer banned the sale of products using angora wool and planned to give its remaining stock of such items to Syrian refugees, according to a Tribune News Service piece, printed in February by *The Gaston Gazette.* "Thanks to Inditex's massive donation, PETA is able to send a vital message about compassion for animals this winter— that only people lacking basic necessities have any excuse for wearing fur that is ripped out of live animals' bodies," Ingrid said.

In March, *The Sitka Daily Sentinel* ran an Associated Press piece, reporting on the decision made by Ringling Bros. and Barnum & Bailey Circus, to phase out the use of elephants in performances. "For 35 years, PETA has protested Ringling Bros.' cruelty to elephants," Ingrid said. "We know extreme abuse to these majestic animals occurs every single day, so if Ringling is really telling the truth about ending this horror, it will be a day to pop the champagne corks, and rejoice." Still, she insisted the circus should stop exploiting the elephants immediately, not later.

Later that month, in a column published by *The Appeal-Democrat,* Ingrid took aim at the no-kill movement, claiming it was based on wishful thinking. "PETA works to stop the killing of all animals, for food, clothing, experimentation and more, but we can't—and won't—turn our backs on dogs and cats in danger of being tossed out or whose owners can't afford costly euthanasia services," she wrote. "To us, the choice is obvious. A humane death is better than a slow and painful one."

Jane Velez-Mitchell suggested animal activists who criticized PETA's sheltering position had inadvertently absorbed talking points from enemies of nonhuman progress. "That whole argument has been put forward by the people who are fronts for industries that are exploiting animals," she told this writer. "The sad fact is that some people in the movement buy the fake news, just like people who are watching a certain channel."

In April, the *No Cages* blog posted an unsigned entry, blasting PETA for sending Pamela Anderson to tour the Maricopa County Jail, after Sheriff Joe Arpaio switched prisoners to a vegetarian diet. "'Sheriff Joe' has been widely criticized for racial profiling of Latinos, racist discrimination against inmates, abuse of power, illegal arrests and deplorable conditions in jail, including numerous wrongful deaths under his watch," the entry stated. "While Arpaio's specific form of racist abuse makes PETA and Anderson's gesture of support particularly egregious, support for any jail or prison is problematic for an organization promoting veganism from an animal rights perspective."

The Baytown Sun printed an article in June, about an investigation into an alligator farm, following allegations from Ingrid's group of criminal abuse there. "PETA's exposé of Hermès suppliers in the U.S. and Africa reveal every Hermès watchband or Birkin bag means a living, feeling being experienced a miserable life and a ghastly death," Ingrid said. "People pay thousands of dollars for such accessories, but the reptiles on these cruel and disgusting factory farms are paying the real price."

In August, *The Beckley Register-Herald* ran a column by Ingrid, addressing the killing of Cecil the lion, a case which inspired surprisingly widespread public outrage. "The details of what took place are appalling, but while it is unusual for the animal to be so well known, do not think for a second that what I'm about to describe constitutes unusual conduct for the pathetic white men who go to Africa and elsewhere to gun down wildlife," Ingrid said, before recounting the details of Cecil's death. "The US and Europe need to ban the importation of heads, horns, feet, and other trophies—pronto."

The next day, Ingrid's organization posted a blog entry on its website, celebrating a court's decision to strike down Idaho's statute that more-or-less criminalized whistleblowing in the agriculture industry. "PETA worked with the Animal Legal Defense Fund, the American Civil Liberties Union of Idaho and the Center for Food Safety to challenge the law, and the court determined that it violates the First and 14th amendments to the U.S. Constitution, which guarantee the right to free speech and to protection from state laws that infringe on personal freedom," Michelle Kretzer wrote. "The decision marks the first time that a court has declared an 'ag-gag' statute unconstitutional."

A few days later, *The Burlington Times* published a Tribune News Service piece, highlighting Ingrid's reaction to a lost Dr. Seuss book—that had recently been found and published—about visiting a pet store. The book came with an addendum, urging readers to adopt animals. "The Seuss books are beloved and rightly beloved, but I'm concerned that this will do much more harm than good unless parents and teachers and adults are careful to use it as a learning exercise," Ingrid explained. "There should have been a disclaimer that said wild birds do not make good pets, they do not belong in cages. If you want to adopt, choose a rabbit or a puppy at a shelter and leave exotics and leave wildlife alone."

Later in August, Reuters posted a story on its website, about Patagonia's decision to stop purchasing wool from a network of Argentinian farms. This followed PETA's release of footage showing workers, at the sites in question, "slashing and stabbing lambs with knives," according to journalist Marty Graham. Ingrid acknowledged the decision was ultimately insufficient. "PETA praises the new move, as 'all steps are good steps,' but cautions that as Patagonia delves deeper into the wool supply chain, it will find that cruelty will always be a part of wool production," she said. "The only one hundred percent humane solution is to switch to all-vegan wool."

Time ran an article on its website, in September, describing a PETA lawsuit that sought to name a monkey as the owner and author of a famous self-portrait. "Naruto took the photo by pressing a button on a camera set up by British nature photographer David Slater, who later used it in a book *Wildlife Personalities*," reporter Tanya Basu. "The macaque lives among a protected colony of other macaques on the Indonesian island of Sulawesi." PETA's organizational chronology heralded this as a groundbreaking lawsuit.

In October, *The Garden City Telegram* printed a Tribune News Service piece, regarding Zimbabwe's decision not to prosecute the Minnesota dentist who killed Cecil the lion. Ingrid—while no doubt disappointed—appeared to look on the bright side. "We're encouraged that Walter Palmer lost business, lost his reputation, and probably lost more in the bargain," she was quoted as saying. "Cecil's death sent a strong message to wildlife slayers that their days are numbered."

In November, *The Times of India* covered an upcoming protest, which would feature Ingrid in a bloodied chicken costume. "When it comes to joy, love, pain, and suffering, chickens feel the same as any cow or human," she said. "PETA points out that an estimated quarter of a million once living, feeling chickens are killed to be eaten every hour in India. We can stop the immense suffering of these gentle birds simply by choosing vegan meals."

Pressure from Ingrid's organization led the American military to cut ties with Deployment Medicine International—a company which committed horrendous acts of animal abuse—according to a blog entry that ran on PETA's website later that month. "The U.S. government has banned DMI from receiving any contracts for the next 15 years," Michelle wrote. "The federal government had been DMI's largest client, awarding it more than $10 million in contracts in recent years, but the disgraced company will now likely be hard-pressed to find customers to pay it to torment animals."

In December, *The Lewiston Sun Journal* reported the local government sought to keep squirrels away from its Christmas tree after the animals chewed on the lights. "Earlier this week, the city took Modern Pest Services up on its offer to install a nearly $1,000 Tree-Shock System at no cost to Lewiston to discourage the squirrels," journalist Kathryn Skelton wrote. "Colton Tlumac, the general manager of the Wildlife Division at Modern Pest, said the zapper system is endorsed by the U.S. Humane Society because it doesn't harm the squirrels in any way." Presumably, he meant lasting harm.

According to the same piece, PETA wanted to feed the squirrels. It's unclear whether this action was meant to replace the Tree-Shock System, or merely to prevent animals from coming in contact with it. "I'd like to offer an opportunity to spread the yuletide spirit to all members of your community regardless of species and cheer up the people who felt their holiday spirit go flat after a recent decision by the city," Ingrid wrote in a letter to the mayor. "As squirrels are curious, clever beings, we propose to give them a holiday gift that would keep them away from the tree as well as fill their bellies: a stash of squirrel-friendly foods, such as acorns and other nuts."

That same day, PETA published a blog post, announcing the National Institutes of Health was ending a project involving maternal-deprivation experiments. "PETA's effort to stop baby monkeys from being terrorized and tortured at NIH included colorful protests, hard-hitting advertising campaigns, a disruption of an NIH seminar, and even a D.C.-wide guerrilla street art installation," Michelle noted. "More than a quarter million PETA supporters wrote to and called government officials to plead with them to take action."

17

NOT A TEA PARTY

USA Today reported in January of 2016 that Ringling Bros. and Barnum & Bailey Circus had moved up the retirement date of its performing elephants. Ingrid was skeptical of the circus' decision to relocate the animals to its own Center for Elephant Conservation. "PETA warns that because the circus has refused to retire these elephants to an accredited sanctuary, vigilance will be needed to determine how they are treated," she said, adding the circus should end all its animal acts.

In March, PETA issued a press release, congratulating Delta for banning companion animals from its cargo holds. "PETA's files are full of cases in which beloved dogs and cats who were transported in airplane cargo holds escaped onto the tarmac, froze to death in transit, or were injured or killed by falling baggage on turbulent flights," Ingrid said. "Delta's compassionate new policy recognizes that dogs and cats are members of the family, not pieces of luggage."

According to an article published later that month by *The San Diego Union-Tribune*, SeaWorld announced it was no longer breeding orcas—making those currently held by the company the last of its killer whales. "PETA has campaigned hard and today there is a payoff for future generations of orcas," Ingrid said. "For decades orcas, dolphins, beluga whales, seals, and many other animals have suffered in SeaWorld confinement, and to do right by them now, SeaWorld must open the tanks to ocean sanctuaries so that these long-suffering animals may have some semblance of a life outside their prison tanks."

Still in March, PETA India posted a blog entry, describing how that country would no longer require duplicative animal testing.

"Following appeals from PETA India and Union Minister Maneka Gandhi, the Ministry of Health & Family Welfare has passed an amendment to Schedule Y of the Drugs and Cosmetics Rules 1945, which spares animals [from] testing for new drug registrations when complete data from earlier toxicity experiments already exist for drugs approved abroad," the unsigned entry stated.

In April, *The Batemans Bay Post* reported PETA claimed to have sent prophylactics to organizers of a hunting festival. "PETA distributed the condoms with one aim: to encourage hunters to stop reproducing," Ingrid said. "Hardly any kids hunt these days. If PETA's condoms have prevented even one more wretched hunter from being born, we have succeeded in saving the lives of deer, birds, and other living things."

PETA published a blog entry in May, highlighting an accolade Ingrid had received. "In an effort to bring together the brightest minds in the global anti-speciesism movement, honor their achievements, and create a more unified force for social change, a group headed by Dr. Walter Neussel last year established the Peter Singer Prize for Strategies to Reduce the Suffering of Animals," Michelle wrote. "It chose the award's namesake as the first recipient. And this year, as the second recipient, it elected PETA President and co-founder Ingrid Newkirk."

Peter Singer played a role in the decision. "Dr. Walter Neussel, who's the person who set it up and largely has financed it, consults with me about the awardees that he or his committee are considering," the philosopher told this author. "Ingrid—I think—was the most obvious candidate." But he suggested this might not have been the case under different circumstances. "Had Henry Spira still been alive, I think he would have been a very clear candidate as well," Peter said. "He was a master strategist in terms of helping animals."

Melanie Joy hosted the prize ceremony with her husband. "I wrote a little talk about her," she said in an interview with this writer, referring to Ingrid. "I shared my story with having met her—not knowing it was her in the van that day." Neal Barnard attended the event. "He was in Berlin for the Peter Singer Prize, and with us all at dinner," Melanie recalled, adding she didn't know anything about the relationship between him and Ingrid.

Jonathan Balcombe, who worked for some time at the Physicians Committee for Responsible Medicine, was shocked by how few people knew about Ingrid and Neal's relationship. "They seem to be a really good match," he told this author. "I think they have a mutual understanding. Maybe to their benefit, they don't live in the same place. Ingrid's office is based in Norfolk, Virginia and Neal Barnard is in Washington, D.C. So that may be ideal for their very, very committed approaches. Both of those people are 24/7 on the go."

In July, Ingrid gave a speech at the Animal Rights National Conference, slamming evaluation groups that—because of the large number of animals involved—sought to focus movement attention on factory farming. "They say suffering is a question of math," Ingrid said, in a recording of her presentation on PETA's YouTube channel. "Animals aren't numbers. They're individuals. Vivisectors reduce animals to numbers." She continued, defending her organization's efforts to save particular nonhumans.

Jon Bockman understandably took Ingrid's speech as an attack on his organization, Animal Charity Evaluators. "There are likely donors who have come to PETA and asked about the recommendations that ACE makes, and why PETA is not on the list of recommended charities," he told this writer. "We're, by and large, saying that if you want to have the greatest impact, you should spend more time on these specific areas. That's not what PETA is doing."

Following the conference, Bockman reached out to Ingrid. "I did write her a series of emails afterward, just to try and start a conversation," he said in an interview with this author. "We did have a number of exchanges—with me trying to kind of explain our position." But nothing productive came of the communication. "PETA has a standard letter that they send to donors [who ask about ACE]," Bockman said, adding the text was riddled with inaccuracies. "It's pretty insulting."

While not directly addressing whether PETA should focus on factory farming, Jonathan Balcombe was sympathetic to the organization's efforts to save individual animals. "As a writer, I've learned that we love stories," he said. "I think there's a lot to be said for focusing on the one elephant—even though the campaign is to get all elephants out of all circuses, or whatever the issue is. By focusing on one particular story, you can really captivate the public. Social movements benefit from diversity. We need different styles. We need lots of different doors for people to go through. PETA has certainly provided a door that's appealing to a lot of people."

Following reports of sexual assault and rape during the festival, Ingrid called for the Running of the Bulls to be banned, according to an August press release on PETA UK's website. "The crystal-clear link between violence to women and cruelty to animals is cause enough to shut down Pamplona's barbaric bullfights and related events," she said. "PETA joins advocates around the world in calling on Pamplona to ban this cruel blood sport and the bloodlust-fueled sexual violence that goes along with it."

Later that month, *The Washington Examiner* covered a recurring problem. "PETA scolded the Park Service Friday over the treatment of fish on Washington's National Mall, after two weeks of scorching temperatures led to a massive fish kill there," journalist John Siciliano wrote. "The group said the Park Service knew of the risks in 2013 when thousands of fish died in the same pond due to prolonged high temperatures." Ingrid pushed the government not to acquire new animals. "PETA is urging the National Park Service, which admits that this pond has been a death trap for fish since it was built in 1976, to stop restocking it," she said.

In September, *The Burlington Post* reported on the upcoming trial of Anita Krajnc—the founder of Toronto Pig Save—who was charged with criminal mischief for giving water to animals on their way to a slaughterhouse. "No one should be penalized for showing mercy to terrified, dehydrated, suffering pigs," Ingrid was quoted as saying. "PETA will be outside the courthouse to remind the world that what animals need is more kind people like Anita Krajnc."

As the presidential election neared, Ingrid's organization launched an advertisement campaign inspired by the infamous Access Hollywood tape. "PETA is using Donald Trump's 'grab em' by the pussy' quote to help cats get adopted in New York City," journalist Joshua Axelrod wrote in an October article, published by *The Washington Examiner*. "In the video released last week, Trump was seen bragging about how his celebrity allows him to do whatever he wants to women, including grabbing them 'by the pussy.'"

The same *Washington Examiner* article featured Ingrid's justification for the campaign, in which she seemed almost apologetic. "The sensationalism of this election has rendered many other important issues invisible," PETA's co-founder said. "We hope this ad will encourage people to think for a second about the crisis facing cats and other animals and—if they have the time, love, patience and funds to do so—to consider opening their homes to one or two beautiful cats from a shelter."

In November, *The Times of India* highlighted a protest against religious exploitation of animals. "Wearing grey clothing to resemble an elephant, Newkirk was 'chained' inside a decorated structure resembling the pillars of a temple and 'beaten' by a mahout using an 'ankus,'" Singh wrote. "Beside her, a display sign read, 'For God's Sake: Stop Chaining Elephants.' She decided to travel to India after watching two documentaries about the plight of captive elephants in the country." One must assume Ingrid acting as the face of such protests made them less effective, given the colonial history of her native Britain.

The PETA International Science Consortium was funding non-animal antitoxin research, according to a press release, uploaded later that month to PETA's website. "Each year, thousands of horses are used as living factories to produce antitoxins," the release said. "These antitoxins are isolated from horses' blood after repeatedly injecting them with toxins, such as diphtheria toxin. Many of these horses are kept on farms in India, where recent inspections uncovered rampant negligence and inadequate veterinary care." PETA was hoping to end this exploitation of horses.

In December, *The Australian Broadcasting Corporation* ran a story online—about the successful prosecution of a shearer, whose illegal abuse of animals was exposed in a PETA video. "The offender was sentenced, without conviction, to a good behavior bond and disqualified from shearing, or managing any farm animals, for two years," journalist Danielle Grindlay wrote. "Agriculture Victoria senior veterinarian Robert Suter said he was confident another five shearers, allegedly depicted in the same video montage released by PETA in July 2014, would be brought to justice."

Later that month, Ingrid's organization published a blog post, regarding a decision made by the National Processed Raspberry Council and the Washington Red Raspberry Commission, ending the groups' support for animal testing. "PETA pointed out that these experiments are not only cruel but also bad science," Lindsay

Pollard-Post wrote. "The effects of obesity and the way in which glucose is regulated are very different in mice and rats compared to humans. And because of vastly different physiologies, any antioxidant or anti-inflammatory effects of raspberries observed in experiments on animals most likely couldn't be applied to humans."

In January of 2017, *The New York Daily News* ran a column by Ingrid, reacting to the bombshell announcement that Ringling Bros. and Barnum & Bailey Circus was closing. "Ringling could not ignore the protesters outside every show, the dwindling attendance, and society's new vision of wildlife, which excludes a person with a whip forcing tigers to jump through hoops and elephants in headdresses being made to stand on a tiny drum out of fear of prodding from the bullhook," she wrote. "It finally recognized that such shows of human domination over nature and its inhabitants belong in the past."

Responding to pressure from Ingrid's organization, a multinational pharmaceutical company agreed not to kill nonhumans while training sales staff, according to a February blog post on PETA's website. "This commitment comes after PETA uncovered evidence that the company was using live animals to demonstrate invasive medical-device procedures," Kretzer wrote. "We demanded that Sanofi join the Cleveland Clinic as well as Johnson & Johnson, Medtronic, and many other surgical-device manufacturers that we've persuaded to switch to advanced human-patient simulators, 'living' human-cadaver models, or synthetic soft-tissue models."

In April, PETA published a blog post, highlighting the animal group's donation of eight surgical simulators—valued at $200,000—to facilities in the developing world. "Bangladesh, Ghana, Jamaica, and Kenya will now use the TraumaMan simulator instead of animals to train doctors in their American College of Surgeons (ACS) sponsored Advanced Trauma Life Support (ATLS) program," the unsigned post stated. "TraumaMan—whose manufacturer, Simulab Corporation, collaborated with PETA on the donation—is ACS-approved as a replacement for animal use in ATLS training. It replicates a breathing, bleeding human torso with realistic skin, tissue, ribs, and internal organs."

Later that month, Ingrid's organization posted a blog entry, announcing the Royal Australasian College of Surgeons would no longer exploit animals in educational exercises. "RACS President

Philip Truskett confirmed the group's decision after our campaign prompted him to study advanced human-simulation technology," the unsigned entry stated. "By the end of this year, RACS will phase out the use of live animals for its Early Management of Severe Trauma program, which trains both civilian physicians and Australian Defence Force medical officers in treating traumatic injuries."

The Coast Guard temporarily halted its use of nonhumans during medical instruction, according to a blog update that PETA ran near the end of April. "Following pressure from PETA and U.S. Rep. Lucille Roybal-Allard (D-Calif.), the U.S. Coast Guard has become the first branch of the military to suspend the shooting, stabbing, and killing of animals in trauma training drills while it studies available human simulators and other non-animal training methods that could be used instead," Kretzer wrote. "The Coast Guard confirmed that the moratorium came into effect after a PETA exposé prompted an official review by the agency."

In May, *The Orange County Register* covered Ingrid's support for local festivities. "Councilman John Stephens got a surprise $5,000 donation toward his proposed July Fourth celebration from PETA, which endorsed his idea of hosting a silent fireworks display," reporter Louis Casiano wrote. "The council on April 18 unanimously endorsed Stephens' idea for the event, but with the condition that he raise [$50,000] from private sources by the May 16 council meeting." Of course, loud fireworks caused animals severe distress. "More dogs run away on the Fourth of July than on any other date, and animal shelters report an increase in the number of lost dogs and cats following fireworks displays," Ingrid said.

Later that month, *The Jerusalem Post* reported Israel was requiring kosher slaughterhouses to change their practices. "The New Guidelines for Humane Kosher Slaughter, published by the Agriculture Ministry's Israeli Veterinary Services and Animal Health office, will effectively eliminate the 'shackle-and-hoist' method of slaughter for any meat coming into Israel as of next year," journalist Sharon Udasin wrote, adding the decision came after PETA conducted an undercover investigation with the help of two Israeli groups.

Still in May, Ingrid's organization posted a blog entry, which seemed to hint at PETA's power of intimidation. "Just weeks after PETA contacted House Foods to ask it to stop conducting experiments on animals, the company put an end to its long-standing practice of force-feeding mice and injecting them with chemicals to make health claims about its products," Katherine Sullivan wrote. "After learning from PETA that experiments on animals are cruel, not required by law, and irrelevant to humans, House Foods executives quickly agreed to ban these archaic tests. We applaud the company for embracing modern, animal-free methods."

For the first time, the Food and Drug Administration accepted the use of human volunteers in lubricant testing, according to a June blog post on PETA's website. "When we asked FDA officials if lubricant companies could test their products on human volunteers instead of animals, they said that it had never been tried before but that they would consider it," the unsigned post stated. "So we asked our friends at Good Clean Love if they would give it a shot, and they jumped at the opportunity." PETA described the FDA's acceptance of the test results as a precedent-setting win.

Later that month, Ingrid's organization ran a blog entry, discussing a donation—by PETA International Science Consortium—of four inhalation-testing machines to various laboratories. "The devices, made by Germany-based manufacturer VITROCELL, test for the health effects of inhaled substances using human lung cells in a dish," Kretzer wrote, adding the items cost $400,000. "Since the machines can use human cells, scientists get a much better idea of how human lungs respond to airborne substances than they can by forcing animals to inhale chemicals."

In July, *National Public Radio* published an article on its website, about a federal judge striking down a Utah law which criminalized whistleblowing in the agricultural industry. "The challenge to Utah's ban was filed by the Animal Legal Defense Fund, PETA, and Amy Meyer, the director of the Utah Animal Rights Coalition," journalist Bill Chappell wrote. "Meyer was arrested in 2013 while she filmed workers using heavy machinery to move a sick cow at a slaughterhouse in Draper City. At the time, Meyer was on public property; the charges against her were later dismissed."

That same month, *The Wall Street Journal* covered an underground action. "Tens of thousands of minks—valued at about

$750,000—were released by vandals from a Minnesota fur farm earlier this week," reporter Quint Forgey wrote. Ingrid empathized with the activists involved. "When the law does so little to protect minks and other animals from a horrifying life of misery on fur farms, it's not hard to understand why some people are compelled to take matters into their own hands and free animals from this kind of grotesque confinement," she said.

In August, *The Bangor Daily News* reported PETA hoped to receive author E.B. White's farmhouse, which was being sold for $3.7 million, as a gift. The group sought to turn the location into what it described as an empathy museum. "E.B. White's portrayal of a pig named Wilbur inspired people all over the world to take a closer look at the animals they consider to be 'food' and go vegan," Ingrid said. "A PETA museum in his historic farmhouse would help visitors see that every pig is 'some pig,' an intelligent individual and not a collection of sausages, bacon, and chops."

Later that month, *The Boston Globe* published a piece about a bull who escaped from a livestock auction. "PETA is calling on the owners to allow this spirited animal to live out his days in peace—and Farm Sanctuary and Skylands Animal Sanctuary & Rescue are ready to take him in," Ingrid said. "No animal should be killed and hacked apart for the fleeting taste of brisket or burgers, and anyone who cares about this bull can help more than 100 animals like him every year simply by going vegan."

Not one to ask others to do something she wasn't willing to do herself, Ingrid was featured in a provocative advertisement, according to an August press release on PETA UK's website. "Stark naked and hanging from a meat hook between the bodies of slaughtered pigs in an ad shot in Spitalfields meat market, PETA founder and Surrey native Ingrid Newkirk will stare down from a billboard circling The Big Meat festival this weekend," the release stated.

Ingrid highlighted the similarities between pigs and humans. "If most people stood inside a slaughterhouse, as I've done, and watched life after life being violently snuffed out, they'd lose their appetite for these wonderful animals' flesh," she said in the same press release. "PETA reminds everyone that our own flesh not only looks like pigs' but tastes like theirs, and no one should celebrate events that involve the torment and death of them and other living beings."

Ingrid argued peace began at the breakfast table, according to a September article in *The Jerusalem Post*. "This is not a simplistic statement," she said. "How can we expect to have peace if we ourselves are putting animals through a slaughterhouse? They are fellow living beings like us, and if we can't understand that, how can we expect to have a greater understanding of other people in the world? So I encourage everybody, use your power, use your voice, be the person you want to be."

In the same article, Ingrid praised consumption habits in the country. "The upsurge of vegan eating in Israel is very, very strong," she told reporter Sarah Levi. "Israel is a leader in the switch to vegan eating, vegetarian foods, for animals but also for the environment; there is a huge environmental consciousness." Ingrid seemed unsurprised by this. "There is a wealth of wonderful, wonderful fresh produce that the rest of the world is envious of, as well as delicious foods readily available," she said. "Tasty vegan food like hummus, falafel, and tahina—which were once regional specialties have now proliferated the global food market and have become mainstream."

Dylan Powell, the co-founder of Marineland Animal Defense, took issue with this sort of narrative. "Israelis consume 102 kg [of meat] per capita—that is more than Canada (92), more than the UK (82), well above any other country in the region and well above the world average (42) and the EU average (82)," he wrote in a 2015 blog post on his website. "If Israel is the 'most vegan country in the world' then advocates should really begin to question just what veganism is and why it is important. If the term can so easily be co-opted to excuse human genocide and apartheid then maybe it is time to rethink our goals, strategies, and effectiveness."

Still in September 2017, Ingrid addressed thousands of activists at an animal-rights march in Tel Aviv. "Our cause—all of ours—is not a tea party," she said in a recording of the event uploaded to PETA's YouTube channel. "It's not a hobby. It's a revolution. Let's pledge today to leave our comfort zone. There is no glory in being comfortable. Change comes from discomfort zones. Let's pledge never to be silent."

Koby Barak—the co-founder of SuperMeat, an Israeli startup developing in-vitro animal products—met Ingrid at the march. "I saw her, approached her and talked for a few minutes with her," he recalled in an interview with this writer, noting Ingrid had heard of SuperMeat. "She told me that she is very supportive of this initiative, and thinks it can make an incredible change for the animals, the ecology, and humankind."

In October, *The London Telegraph* reported a luxury brand was eliminating fur from its collections. "After more than twenty years of PETA protests against Gucci's kangaroo-fur loafers and seal-fur boots, Gucci has finally pledged to join Armani, Ralph Lauren, and Stella McCartney in the ranks of fur-free fashion houses," Ingrid said. "The writing was on the wall: Today's shoppers don't want to wear the skins of animals who were caged, then electrocuted or bludgeoned to death. Until all animal skins and coats are finally off the racks of clothing stores worldwide, PETA will keep up the pressure on the clothing and fashion industry."

Later that month, *The Washington Post* ran a piece by Ingrid, warning standards of animal care in D.C. were slipping. "Driving down Canal Road, near Fletcher's Boathouse, I saw a large fawn lying on the pavement," PETA's co-founder wrote. "As she flailed, pirouetting into the road and then back to the berm, collapsing to regain her strength and again trying fruitlessly to right herself, I called 911. Animal control promised to send a driver out 'ASAP.' But the deer remained in agony for a full hour."

Ingrid called for mayoral action. "I was told that the District had promised the alliance funding for additional officers and vehicles but has so far failed to deliver and that [Humane Rescue Alliance's] inquiries have gone unanswered for some months now," she wrote in the same piece. "When the citizens, wildlife and other animals of our city run into trouble and cannot help themselves, they count on government services. Don't let them down."

In November, *The Green Bay Press-Gazette* published an article, about PETA's campaign to stop locals from using rat poison. "PETA recommends that residents store garbage in sturdy containers that rats can't chew through; feed pets indoors and pick up their food dishes; trim vegetation around buildings; seal holes, cracks, and gaps on building exteriors that rats can get into; and use live traps to catch any remaining rats," reporter Jonathan Anderson wrote.

Ingrid sought to paint a more sympathetic picture of the vilified species. "Rats are intelligent, affectionate animals who form close bonds with their families and friends, enjoy playing and wrestling, and even giggle when tickled," she said in the same article. "Killing these animals only causes others to move into the newly available spaces, so PETA urges homeowners and building managers to avoid unwanted houseguests entirely by rat-proofing buildings."

18

INDOMITABLE

In March of 2018, *The London Daily Mail* reported singer Barbara Streisand had cloned her dog. While sympathetic, Ingrid criticized the decision. "We all want our beloved dogs to live forever, but cloning doesn't achieve that—instead, it creates a new and different dog," PETA's co-founder said. "When you consider that millions of wonderful adoptable dogs are languishing in animal shelters every year, or dying in terrifying ways when abandoned, you realize that cloning adds to the homeless animal population crisis."

Later that month, *The Dayton Daily News* printed a story about a politician's effort to make Labrador retrievers the official dog of Ohio. Unsurprisingly, Ingrid opposed the effort. "The last thing that Ohio's already severely crowded animal shelters need is a deluge of yet another type of dog," she said. "If Ohioans' hearts are set on naming an official state dog, PETA suggests the humble, healthy, and 100 percent lovable all-American mutt."

PETA planned to rent billboards highlighting Donald Trump Jr.'s involvement in trophy hunting, and call for his deportation, according to an April piece in *The El Paso Times*. The campaign was in response to anti-immigrant hysteria, which had been stirred up by the White House. "When we heard about the National Guard being deployed, you heard this xenophobic reaction about undesirables and that people are just coming into the country to cheat, and steal and be violent," Ingrid said. "It upsets me because it's not right."

Still in April, *The Washington Post* reported on the exploitation of a performing bear at a Russian sporting event. "In addition to being inhumane and utterly out of touch, using a bear as a captive servant to perform at a soccer game is downright dangerous unless, as is often the case, the animal's teeth and claws have been cruelly removed," Ingrid said. "The bear is the symbol of Russia, so we hope the country's people will show some compassion and national pride and stop abusing them. Common decency should compel the soccer league to pull this stunt, which flies in the face of the spirit of fair play."

Near the end of the month, PETA distributed a media statement, celebrating the passage of groundbreaking legislation. "San Francisco has made history as the biggest U.S. city to outlaw fur sales, and that's in large part because of the dedicated efforts of Supervisor Katy Tang," Ingrid said. "Animals have found in her a true ally, and they need all the allies they can get. PETA is happy to honor her for helping to establish a model of compassion for other cities to follow."

In May, *The Wall Street Journal* ran an article about Ingrid's scheduled address to Google workers. "It wasn't until she sat waiting in a parking lot that a call came through notifying her the event was canceled," reporters Kirsten Grind and Douglas MacMillan wrote. "Ms. Newkirk had been invited by some employees to discuss her view that animals can be subject to prejudice just as people can, as part of the company's 'Talks at Google' series. Another group of employees said the topic was offensive to humans who face racism, and they protested."

Later that month, *The Wilmington News Journal* covered PETA's request that Slaughter Beach change its name. "Unfortunately, many people don't look deeply into the origins of words and names, but that doesn't diminish the negative connotations—especially for impressionable young minds—of a word like 'slaughter,' which conjures up images of dead and dying animals," Ingrid said. The vice mayor of Slaughter Beach insisted the town's name had nothing to do with violence against nonhumans.

Still in May, PETA issued a press release, announcing a gift to Prince Harry and Meghan Markle, who were soon to be married. "An Indian bull who was found weak and injured, likely after a lifetime of being forced to toil in the hot sun pulling a heavy cart, has been adopted by [the group's affiliate] on behalf of the happy couple and named Merry—a hybrid of the names Meghan and Harry—in their honor," the release stated. "He'll spend the rest of his days relaxing in peace at a sanctuary in Maharashtra, India."

Ingrid was quoted in the press release. "Prince Harry and Meghan Markle now have a one-ton bull to call their own," she said. "Rescuing Merry is an ideal wedding present for a couple who want their big day to be celebrated with charitable works and contributions. The royal wedding is the perfect time for anyone to spare a thought for and show some love to all our fellow living, feeling beings."

That same day, *USA Today* published a column by Ingrid, slamming a Miami high school for using live animals as props for its jungle-themed prom. "The tiger, a lemur, birds, and an African fennec fox were hauled out amid pounding music, flashing lights, fire dancers, and a crowd of rambunctious teenagers," PETA's co-founder wrote, adding students might not know how lucky they were. "Attacks on humans by captive big cats occur with staggering regularity. Cages cannot contain these apex predators, and captivity is a living hell for them."

As readers approach the date when this book was written, it's worth considering the future of Ingrid's organization and her role in animal-rights history. Without the influence of its indomitable co-founder, will PETA eventually become a shell of its former self? For all the publicity stunts and undercover investigations, might Ingrid be remembered for something unexpected—like championing in-vitro meat? This writer put questions like this to his interviewees.

Over the years, Ingrid has insisted she has no plans to retire. But, like everyone else, she's mortal. So what would her organization look like without her? After all, in the 2003 *New Yorker* profile, she suggested PETA was akin to a benevolent dictatorship. "This is not a democratic organization," she told Michael Specter. "I never pretended that it was. I don't know where exactly it would go if it were a democracy. And I am not willing to give it a try."

In the clear majority of cases, Jon Bockman told this writer, there is an inevitable stagnation when someone leads an organization for 30-40 years. "Bringing in that fresh injection of ideas is just extremely valuable," he said, arguing this generally outweighed the cost of turnover. "All organizations should regularly be thinking about their top leadership . . . There is a danger in becoming too complacent, and just leaving the same person in charge forever."

For his part, Bockman could imagine PETA without Ingrid. "I'm very excited to see what kind of new ideas or approaches they might take," he said in an interview with this writer. "Because at the end of the day, PETA's got a very, very, very well-known brand— the most well known in animal rights. I think that's without debate, at least in the United States. There's just so much good to be done there. So I would love to see what a new person would do with PETA."

According to Kalista Barter, during her tenure at PETA, Tracy Reiman was in line to succeed Ingrid. "Tracy, in general, is more corporate, business-minded than Ingrid," Kalista told this author. "Ingrid comes from an activist background. That's kind of at her core." Kalista envisioned PETA becoming a bit more buttoned-down, like the Humane Society of the United States. "I still think all the stunts and everything would happen," she said. "That's part of PETA." (Attempts to interview Tracy for this book were unsuccessful.)

Dan Mathews didn't know what form PETA would take without Ingrid and was unaware of the organization's plan of succession. But he seemed confident the group would endure. "There are so many incredible programs in place," he said in a discussion with this writer. "The philosophy has been there now for well over three decades. It's anybody's guess, but the staying power is obviously there."

But what about Ingrid's role in history? Peter Singer, often described as the father of the modern animal-rights movement, hailed her contributions to the nonhuman struggle. "I think Ingrid's legacy—the first and foremost thing—is really building a mass movement for animals in the United States and ultimately, of course, helping to spread it worldwide," he said in an interview with this author.

Despite her clashes with Ingrid over the years, Karen Davis seemed to agree with Peter. "Ingrid really launched the animal-rights movement in the United States," Karen told this writer. "There were others who were doing important work, like Cleveland Amory with Fund for Animals. But Cleveland himself wasn't even a vegetarian and they didn't have a vegetarian component of Fund for Animals." Leaders of the old incarnation of the Humane Society of the United

States were no better. "They all ate animals," she continued. "They wouldn't touch the topic."

Matt Ball struck a similar note. "Ingrid was the person who changed the way Americans thought about animals," he said in an interview with this author. "If something happened with animals, people thought PETA. It just came to mind. PETA would be mentioned in late-night talk shows a zillion years ago. Relatively soon after they started, they were masters of getting into the cultural discussion of things and bringing animals into that. I just think that's an amazingly profound legacy."

Speaking with this writer, Josh Harper stressed the boldness of Ingrid's undertaking. "She built an organization in the United States, that if you had asked animal-rights activists in the mid-1970s—if they would ever see the likes of within ten years—they would have laughed at you," the archivist said. "Vegans were having a difficult time even getting a lecture scheduled at a vegetarian conference or getting the Vegan Society to utilize the word animal rights. I don't think they could have imagined such a turn of events as PETA. And I think Ingrid's ambition was largely responsible for that."

The impact of Ingrid's work extended beyond the borders of the United States. "My interests are very international, so I see stuff that PETA is doing in China, in the Philippines, and various other places," Kim Bartlett said in a discussion with this writer. "PETA is opening offices. They get people to do things that are extremely important, in places where animal rights is still not a social issue at all. So I think she's got a huge legacy."

Speaking with this author, Melanie Joy argued Ingrid's leadership was important because PETA's co-founder was one of the few women in a position of power in the nonhuman struggle. "The animal-rights movement, and particularly the vegan movement, is primarily women," Melanie said. "The leadership is primarily men. That unequal distribution mirrors a patriarchal power differential and dynamic that's obviously pervasive in societies around the world. It's deeply problematic." She acknowledged feminist critiques of PETA but insisted this didn't invalidate the importance of female leadership.

Lorri Houston agreed. "Just because PETA does this one thing that you disagree with, it doesn't negate all their other work," she told this author. "It doesn't negate that Ingrid herself is a strong woman and a feminist. That's where I think we should take more of that middle path, and agree where we can agree, and disagree where we don't [agree]—respectfully. Everybody will make their decision. But it's undeniable what PETA has done."

While suggesting reasonable people could disagree about the effectiveness of negative coverage, Ann Chynoweth seemed to admire the strength which allowed Ingrid to weather various media storms. "She got people to pay attention," Ann told this author. "She was willing to make people uncomfortable—even to suffer the slings and arrows for it."

Matt wasn't very sympathetic to criticisms of Ingrid's attention-seeking philosophy. "I think a lot of it is just driven by jealousy," he told this writer. "I think a lot of people wish they were getting media attention and that they were bringing in tens of millions of dollars for their work." While Matt was concerned about vegans' negative public perception, he didn't think Ingrid was necessarily to blame. "I brought this up a couple of time when I've spoken at classes at colleges," he said, mentioning students would tell him why they didn't like vegans. "They say, it's because I met so-and-so and they were a real dick. They don't say, PETA is a bunch of idiots."

Speaking with this author, Chas Chiodo seemed unwilling to look past what he saw as Ingrid's interpersonal failings. "For people who don't know the nasty Ingrid, she's going to go down as the woman who founded the animal-rights movement," he predicted. "I don't think she belongs on a pedestal, because of all the nasty deeds she's done over her life. But if she was a nice person, I'd put her on a pedestal."

Ingrid's relationship with various organizations in the movement was not always constructive. "PETA was not the only game in town in the 1980s," Josh told this writer, suggesting Ingrid worked to undermine groups like Mobilization for Animals and Trans-Species Unlimited. "She saw those organizations as being competition for a limited amount of donor funds. She believed very much that her ideology and her strategies alone were going to be what won victories for animals."

Jim Mason thought Ingrid's views on sheltering had to be considered when assessing her role in the animal movement. "If you're with Best Friends Animal Society—you believe in no-kill and that every life matters—then Ingrid is like Adolf Hitler," he said to this writer. "That was an extremely-passionate controversy that I suppose rages to this day, the kill or no-kill issue. That's got to be one of her legacies. And that's not exactly a happy, positive one."

Ultimately, as Kim noted in an interview with this author, it's impossible to predict how history will judge an individual. "Ingrid's been responsible for some negative things happening, like people dropping out of the cause," the movement journalist said. "There has been negative publicity because Ingrid has insulted reporters or the action has backfired." Still, Kim believed the net effect of Ingrid and PETA's work was overwhelmingly positive. "It's definitely a plus—a big plus," she said. "I think they've been essential."

INDEX

ABOUT THE AUTHOR

Jon Hochschartner lives in Connecticut with his family. He enjoys watching the Knicks and *Ocarina of Time* speedruns. Previously, he wrote *The Animals' Freedom Fighter: A Biography of Ronnie Lee, Founder of the Animal Liberation Front*. Visit his website at Hochschartner.com.

Made in the USA
Middletown, DE
03 April 2020